Be the Bulb!

Why some people shine brighter than others and how you can become one of them.

By Lori Martinek

herlife
publishing, LLC

Published by Herlife Publishing LLC

Copyright ©2009 by Lori Martinek

ISBN   0-979-8034-0-3
ISBN 13   978-0-9798034-0-6

Library of Congress Control Number: 2008941745

Published by Herlife Publishing LLC
Order additional copies at www.herlifepublishing.com

Be the Bulb! Why People Shine Brighter Than Others and How You Can Become One of Them. All rights reserved. No part of this book may be used, reproduced or transmitted in any manner or form or by any means, electronic or mechanical, or by translation into any language, without written permission from the publisher (with the exception of 'fair use' of brief quotations attributed in critical articles and reviews).

For information on foreign, translation or other rights, please contact:
Herlife Publishing LLC
www.herlifepublishing.com

Contact Lori Martinek at
www.herlifepublishing.com
www.pplusonline.com

Cover Design: Cindy Miller Designs
Interior design and production: Cindy Miller Designs
Author Photography: Babe Sarver

Printed in the United State of America

To my father, Eric Kahn, a Holocaust survivor who overcame great odds to journey to America and create a life of opportunity for himself and his family. He encouraged me always and could see my light, even when it did not shine at its brightest.
I miss you, Dad.

To my mother, Florence, who provided a shining example of what a woman can be, without limitations. You always had great faith in me and were never surprised by my success.
Thank you.

To my daughter, Ellie, and my son, Michael. May you find your true light and allow it to shine brightly and strongly, always. I have always seen it in both of you.
Love, Mom

Table of Contents

Unleash the Entrepreneur Within! 1

PART I: Laying the Groundwork
Chapter 1: Be the Bulb, Be the Brand 21
Chapter 2: Understanding Attraction Marketing 31
Chapter 3: Motivational Energy Explained 41

PART II: How To Be The Bulb, Step By Step
Chapter 4: Creating the Source 57
Chapter 5: Turning on the Light 65
Chapter 6: Channeling and Building On Your Light 81

PART III: Putting It To Work: Powerful Strategies To Promote You and Your Company
Chapter 7: Creating a Powerful Brand 87
Chapter 8: Putting Your Brand in the Spotlight 97
Chapter 9: Bright Shining Brand, Step by Step 115

PART IV: Building on Success: Creating Entrepreneurial Synergy
Chapter 10: Keep Your Bulb Shining Brightly and Strong 125
Chapter 11: Be a Good Gatekeeper 135
Chapter 12: Avoid Inertia and Burnout 145
Chapter 13: Create a Chandelier: Make It All Work Together 155

Chapter 14: Epilogue: A Million Watts of Light 163

Be the Bulb!

By Lori Martinek

Unleash The Entrepreneur Within

Why is it that some people just seem to shine brighter than others? How do they always seem to glow with the energy of enthusiasm and excitement, of potential and personality and power?

Who are these people and how are they so often able to see what is possible, to get what they choose to go after and to draw others toward their light? Why are they so often successful entrepreneurs and leaders and mentors? Where do they get their energy, their direction and their drive?

Like moths to a flame, people are drawn to these individuals and their energy. It is positive energy that shines brightly and confidently wherever they go. It is positive energy that fills a room with their presence as they enter and draws others to their side because of how it feels to be near them and with them. It is Inspiring, Empowering, Energizing, Exciting.

You can be one of these people. You can learn to fill a room – and your life – with positive, magnetic energy that attracts the types of people whom you want to be with and work with; the types of customers whom you want to sell to and serve; and the types of people whom you need in your world to feel happy, fulfilled and successful.

You can be the light that attracts others with your energy. You can have the company that potential customers are drawn to first. You can be all of this and more, when you choose to *Be the Bulb!*

And like those moths to a flame, what you seek will not only be apparent, but it will come to you because, possibly for the very first time, you know what you are looking for. Your attention will be focused on what you want and need. You will no longer waste energy on thoughts and actions or circumstances that do not move you toward your goals. You will no longer waste energy on negative people and situations that subtract from your energy rather than add to it. You will no longer spend time on regrets, remorse or ruminations because you will KNOW WHO YOU ARE and WHAT YOU NEED TO DO. You will have the energy and the confidence to actively go after what you want and get it. Sounds good, doesn't it? Here's the best part: You already have everything that you need to get started. You already possess all of the internal resources and capabilities that it takes to *Be the Bulb!*

There is a power within you. It exists within all of us. It is the power to become who and what you want to be and to get everything that you want to have in your life. You possess an inherent ability to take your God-given talents and strengths and convert them into positive energy that can build a business, a rewarding relationship, or a life. Focus on your gifts and more gifts will come your way. Focus on your strongest attributes and you will create confidence. Confidence creates positive energy, and positive energy – when properly targeted and projected – is highly contagious. People will be drawn to your dynamic energy and will want to remain near it, and you. Your professional and personal lives will be filled with the types of people whom you need to realize your plans, your goals and your dreams – whatever they may be. Your energy will continue to build and your light will grow even brighter.

This is primarily a book for entrepreneurs and for those with an entrepreneurial mindset: individuals who own or are about to begin a business, professionals in search of a greater network, and others who want to find the means to put their plans for a more fulfilling or rewarding life to work.

This book is for people who are willing – and ready – to move forward in their lives and for people who are willing to work at it. This book is for people who are looking for recognition, success, financial freedom, personal or professional fulfillment and progress in their lives and careers. It is for small business owners and entrepreneurs who are looking for an 'edge' that can help them be more successful. It is for executives and professionals who are looking to achieve greater visibility and success through a personal marketing plan. This book is also for mid-life career changers and emerging entrepreneurs, many of whom may be Baby Boomers in transition who are now planning their 'next acts'. The concepts and practical advice contained in the pages that follow do not discriminate by age, education, money or any other socio-economic factor. They apply and are accessible to all. There is no financial investment to make. There is no secret to hoard or pyramid to climb. No special educational training or degree is needed. There is nothing to wait for, prepare for or postpone. You already possess everything that you need to put the advice that you will read here to work. There is no reason why you should not begin changing your life *today*.

This book will give you the confidence you need to reach out for success and claim it, and to begin building a business or a new career instead of just talking about it. Your life can be all that you want it to be. Your company can be all that you want it to be. Wanting, however, is only the first step. *You must also have a plan to move forward and you must be willing to work at it.*

This book is that plan. It will teach you how to identify your strengths and set your sights on the goals that are most important to you or your company. It will take you step by step from where you are today through a process that creates and channels positive energy in a manner that will truly get results.

I'm going to introduce you to the concept of Motivational Energy, a powerful combination of personal branding, attraction marketing and promotional principles that have nothing to do with sitting back and wanting and wishing and everything to do with creating success. Motivational Energy is the power source that we all possess but don't always utilize to its fullest potential. Learning to recognize and channel this power is the first step. 'Flipping the Switch' and putting our energy out into the world comes next. Flipping the Switch requires conscious decision and action to get the ball rolling. This is where many of you may have to face your fears in order to move forward. Active Attention then creates momentum. It is what allows your Bulb to burn brightly, and it is what will help you become not just Dynamic, but Brilliant.

Here's part of the reason why it works: If you are focused on living your best life, the best in life will come to you. If you are focused on what you love or love to do, and on what you most want to be or to have, then these are the things that you will pay attention to and these are the things that you will attract more of. You will be open to opportunities that relate to these desires and these parts of your life will grow stronger. If you are focused on being successful, you will be successful. There's nothing magical or mystical about this. Focused, energized people are most often the ones who achieve their goals. Why? Because they are focused on their goals, open to opportunity and apply Active Attention to projecting their energy into the marketplace.

Regardless of what you are looking for, this book will show you how to plug into your Core Strengths and channel your Motivational Energy to light up a room – and your life – and get what you want and need from the world. You will learn how to focus on your strengths and amplify them by creating a personal branding plan and turn your company's strengths into sales success through a magnetic marketing strategy. You will learn how to clarify your goals and identify exactly what and who you need to attract so that you can create a targeted marketing strategy that really works. You will also learn how important good gatekeeping is to ensuring that your efforts are fully productive by keeping the nay-sayers at bay. You will learn how to stay on track and away from people, perhaps even customers, who can hamper your success. You will learn how to create boundaries that don't build walls, and how to fight the inertia that can cause your energy – and your light – to dim over time.

This book is a plan to build on entrepreneurial strengths and to foster entrepreneurial success. It is essential for anyone who is considering starting or buying a business, and it could be a life preserver for someone who is struggling to succeed.

What Creates Entrepreneurial Success

What makes someone a good business person? What does it take to create entrepreneurial success? Passion, and thoughtful tenacity. The confidence to dare, and to succeed, and a willingness to work, very hard, and until the goal is achieved.

That may or may not be the answer you were hoping for. Success, like reality, is something that we have to create for ourselves. True success does not come from wishing and waiting, it comes from wanting it and *working at it*. No one said it would be easy. The most rewarding efforts rarely are. Investing effort gives us a greater appreciation for the results. Success tastes sweetest when we have *earned* it.

Successful entrepreneurs have passion – for their product, their service and their business concept. They believe in something so strongly that they can't wait to get started creating and building. They know in their hearts that they have found a way to do something better, faster, cheaper or in a way that will deliver greater satisfaction than anything else that's in the marketplace right now. They know that their idea is a good one. *They can feel it*. Their confidence is unmistakable.

Ask one of these individuals what they do or what they're working on and they usually dive right into their story. Their excitement is contagious; their commitment obvious. They are smiling, relaxed and positive – and unmistakably passionate about their topic. They love what they do, they love their work and they love to talk about it. You can't help but smile just listening to them.

They know what's at stake and they're willing to work hard to make their business happen. They relish the challenge, whether it's a one-time entrepreneurial undertaking to fulfill a lifelong interest or the thrill of starting, growing and selling the next in a series of successful businesses. These are the folks we call serial entrepreneurs.

What do successful serial entrepreneurs eat for breakfast (or any entrepreneur for that matter)? They begin their days with an element of uncertainty and a willingness to accept risk and responsibility in order to reap the rewards that success can bring. As a long-time business owner, I know that all of the responsibility for the decisions that I make regarding my company rests squarely on my shoulders. I decide what needs to happen and how to make it happen. I accept the risk and the responsibility of my decisions and actions. But all of the rewards are mine as well, and they are not just financial. There is an immense amount of satisfaction involved in creating something successful and in making something good happen. You have to take the risk in order to truly earn the reward, whether it is fame, acclaim, money or some other kind of satisfaction or wealth. You have to be willing to risk something in order to earn something extraordinary, regardless of what extraordinary may mean to you.

That's not to say that you or anyone else should charge off and risk everything on your business idea without having a plan in place to make it happen. Many people have passion. Many people are willing to take risks and work hard to earn rewards. Many people also start a business without taking the time to outline their real goals for their company, develop strategies to achieve those goals or ensure that they have access to all of the resources that they will need to put their plans into action. This is non-productive risk and it will derail your efforts to be successful. Planning is part of the work that must be done. Success is rarely accidental.

That's why I say that thoughtful tenacity is one of the most critical traits that an entrepreneur can possess. Thoughtful tenacity is the ability to think through your decisions before you jump into them and to follow a plan with flexibility. Thoughtful tenacity requires you to re-think and re-plan as needed, and to be willing to do it over and over again, if necessary. When circumstances change, a new opportunity arises or things just don't work out as anticipated or planned, a true entrepreneur thinks it through first and *then* makes the next decision – and the next and the next – until the goal is reached and that task has been completed successfully. Instinct should be a factor, knee jerking should not. Knee jerking is reaction without thought and it is usually more disruptive than productive. Thoughtful tenacity relies on information, instinct and flexibility. It gets the job done and it requires discipline.

Do you have what it takes to be a successful entrepreneur? Do you have the attitude, the aptitude and the fortitude that must accompany a good idea, a great business plan and adequate resources? Do you have a true appreciation for the amount of planning and work that has to goes into the effort? Are you excited by the challenge?

And do you understand now why successful entrepreneurs are usually smiling? They know the enormity of the task that they have undertaken, they have embraced it wholeheartedly and they are energized by knowing – actually feeling – that they can succeed. They are confident and it shows in their attitude and their work. Their positive energy is apparent to everyone they meet.

And energy has everything to do with *Being the Bulb!*

I am going to teach you about a concept called Attraction Marketing, which is a strategy for putting yourself and your products into the marketplace in a way which brings you exactly what you need to succeed. Putting your energy into the marketplace in a focused, positive manner will attract the kinds of people and customers that you want in your world and the opportunities that you need to sell, serve and succeed. Attraction Marketing is all about others being attracted to the positive energy of your message, the energetic tone of your branding and the momentum that circulates around you. It is about shining brightly with a light that pulls people toward you and your energy.

When we channel our authentic energy and target it in a focused manner at a specific audience or goal, we call attention to our light. Focus and attention cause our Bulb – our light – to burn even more brightly. When our Bulbs burn brightly, we attract what we want and need out of life, whether it is product success, personal success or professional success. The brighter we shine, the more we attract. *Put it out there, and pull it back.* What we put into the marketplace is what we will attract back. It's as simple – and as complicated – as that.

There is nothing mystical or magical about any of this. Attraction Marketing is a strategy for creating personal and product success through authentic, strength-based branding, targeted messaging, active effort and social marketing models that redefine traditional marketing concepts. It is based on the concept of Motivational Energy, which is essential to entrepreneurial success. Attraction Marketing amps up the energy that goes into your effort and moves you closer to your goals faster by targeting your energy and your effort in a focused and appropriate direction. It outshines traditional marketing theories and puts all those wishing and wanting scenarios to shame. Why? Because it is understandable, accessible and achievable – and it is applicable to any part of your life. *You can do this.*

Some people are born knowing intuitively how to shine and their light burns very brightly, without apparent effort. Others have studied the process and learned how to turn on their light. Anyone can learn to shine brightly. Anyone can learn to *Be the Bulb!* You can do this, and you should.

Learning how to put Attraction Marketing to work and to *Be the Bulb!* is especially important for people who have chosen to go into business for themselves, for professionals who are searching for new ways to market their services and for anyone who wants to stand out in a crowded marketplace, whether professionally or personally. Let's face it, the Internet has made all of us much more anonymous. We are competing for attention globally as well as locally, and in all types of relationships. Attraction Marketing makes us more visible, so that we stand out from the crowd.

Attraction Marketing will help you shine, but you have to choose to put it to work.

Why We Choose To Be Entrepreneurs

Why does someone choose to become an entrepreneur? We do it for the opportunity to act on an idea or a dream, to make a living from what we love to do, to build something that wasn't there before and to watch it grow. We do it for the flexibility and the control, the creativity and the chaos. There is no one reason and there are a thousand reasons. Entrepreneurship is like that. There is nothing that is 'one size fits all' about it. And really, isn't that the point of why we love it in the first place? Entrepreneurs are rebels and rule breakers at heart. We are daring and disciplined, all at the same time. We really don't make the best 'corporate citizens'. We want to make things happen …. *now*.

I firmly believe that entrepreneurship is something that chooses you. The elements of successful entrepreneurship are part of our psychological makeup from the start. If you were the six-year-old who had the lemonade stand, the eight-year-old who produced neighborhood plays or the ten-year-old who sold family treasures at a yard sale (sometimes without the owners' knowledge), you know what I'm talking about. If you were the college student who organized the study group, the parent who recruited for the fund-raising project or the adult who is the most likely to start a new networking or social group, you know what I mean. Entrepreneurs, by nature, are doers and creators, not joiners. We often join the corporate world early in our careers but, just as often, we eventually opt out. Some evacuate immediately while others need more time, but true entrepreneurs all jump ship eventually. We have no choice. Corporate environments were not created for us. There is too much structure and not enough flexibility, too little creativity and far too little room for risk taking. We feel like we are working by rote. We become bored out of our minds, and frustrated, quickly.

I was never a good corporate employee, and I say that with pride. I excelled at my work, exceeded all expectations and goals, and set new standards for quality and enthusiasm. At the same time, I was continually looking for ways to improve the process. I was bored by the pace, frustrated by the bureaucracy and amazed at much of the incompetence (or at least apathy) that I saw on a daily basis (and sometimes reported to). I also found structured hours to be both limiting and suffocating. Nine to five never worked well for me. Don't get the wrong idea. I work at least 50 hours a week, almost every week, but they are my hours and structured to match my rhythms and my energy. I am a (very) early morning person who is highly productive at a time of day when many people are still just thinking about starting their day. I learned early in my career that you can't begin your corporate job at 5 or 6 a.m. (although I have gone to the office that early and it's a great time to get things done). Well you can, but they tend to frown on it (no one else is there to see you working) and you certainly don't get any credit for it. You are still expected to be there until (at least) five at night, regardless of what time you came in, how much work you completed or whether or not there is anything remaining for you to do. I never, ever could understand the logic of forcing this structure on anyone except the employee who is responsible for answering the phones (which is now mostly automated) or the customer service department, which is often staffed by a (remote) 24-hour call center.

I made it about ten years before I threw in the towel on the corporate employee game and started my own team. I have never regretted that move and know, without question, that starting my own business was the single best choice that I have made in my business life.

There's definitely something about entrepreneurship that gets in your blood. It has now been more than 20 years since I worked for a company that I did not own, and I have been a full or partial owner of at least five other companies during the same two decades that my marketing and PR firm has been in existence. I am currently the owner and principal of that firm, a speaker and author and the owner of a small publishing company. I am energized by the variety and the challenge, and I greet each new day with excitement and enthusiasm. Why? Because I work in a reality that I created and it fits my talents – and my personality – to a tee.

I am very fortunate to have found this out early in my career, when I was just entering my thirties. I have always been proud of myself for having the courage to 'take the plunge', start my own company and become my own boss – and even prouder for my ability to stick with it and succeed at it. When you create something, it is truly yours to point to.

Once you've owned a business, it is difficult to even imagine working as an employee again. I love having clients and commitments and an action-packed calendar, but I also thrive on the freedom and the flexibility, the purpose and the potential, the risk and the reward and yes, even the uncertainty, that owning my own company provides to me. Sure, it would be nice to have better health insurance or some of the other benefits that you often get when you work for 'someone else', but even those perks aren't as abundant (or assured) as they used to be. I am not willing to pay the price of having traditional benefits (and I'm not talking about the price of the premiums) by trading away any of the less tangible perks of entrepreneurship. Why? *Because the other side of uncertainty is potential.* Entrepreneurs know that they have the potential to create success, even greatness, and the potential to do that is very sexy and very intoxicating. We do not see limitations on our ability to realize our full potential. Our glasses are not only half full, they're constantly being replenished.

I am one of those people who needs to call the shots, take the risks and yes, accept the responsibility (and the rewards!) of my decisions. I am a serial entrepreneur. I had the lemonade stand, wrote and produced the neighborhood play with my best friend in the third grade, organized fundraisers for the elementary school PTA while my children were in school and raised major money for the local education foundation. The list goes on and on and today I operate three businesses, each within its own set of risks and rewards (you're reading one of them). Knowing that I am responsible for my own success and that I can – and have – made it happen time and time again is all that I need to start my day with a smile on my face.

The fact that you are now reading this book tells me that you likely also possess an entrepreneurial mindset. How do you know for sure?

Entrepreneurs are visionaries and organizers, planners and doers. They have ideas that they are willing, and able, to act on. They also exist in the corporate world, but they are putting their efforts into someone else's products or mission, and on behalf of someone else's dreams and goals. At some point, the frustration of that becomes apparent and they long to go out on their own. You may be feeling this kind of frustration right now.

Deciding what you will do and how you will feed your entrepreneurial passion are the two of the most important decisions that you will make in your entrepreneurial life. It's not 'Why do I want to start a business?' but 'What do I want to build my business from or around, and how do I choose the best path to follow (or forge!)?' Answering these questions will guide your success.

There are hundreds of books and organizations that exist to provide entrepreneurs and would-be entrepreneurs with step by step advice on how to start and build a business. These are sources of very valuable and important information that can improve the chances of your success – once you have answered the real question: 'What do I want my business to be and why am I choosing this path over something else?'

Improving Your Chances For Success

How we choose the type of business we begin will have a huge influence on whether or not we are successful. Here's why: Passion comes from interest and engagement. When we are doing something that we have a true interest in, when we are doing something that we are good at or eager to learn about, when we are doing something that gets and holds our interest and makes the hours fly by, that is engagement. That is passion. *Passion is the absolute must-have ingredient in any successful business undertaking.* You must be passionate about what you do and a have a genuine desire, and a huge enthusiasm, to share that passion for your business with others, whether they are potential customers or just innocent bystanders to your excitement.

Passion is what gets you leaping out of bed in the morning to get to work so that you can immerse yourself in your business and its opportunities and challenges. Passion is what makes you continually redraw that 'line in the sand' that you swore you'd never cross from a time or financial standpoint because you KNOW that you are just inches away from succeeding. Passion is what leads you to hang on just a little bit longer – and often just long enough – to make the difference between a win and a loss. Passion never lets you give up when there is still a new path to discover, another idea waiting outside the box, or even just a hint of a strategy that hasn't been tried before. Passion encourages you to accept the risk and the responsibility, in hopes of a return that goes far beyond financial reward to fulfillment.

Passion is what makes it all seem like fun, rather than work. You've heard it before: If you do what you love, you will never work a day in your life. I am here to tell you that this is one hundred percent absolutely true. And: if you build a business based on what you love and do best, you will be creating a company that is driven by your strengths, your talents and your interests. You will be starting a venture that is truly an extension of you because it is based on your strengths, your talents and your passion: the very best parts of you.

You will be doing your life's work instead of just working for a living and, no matter how challenging or difficult it may seem at any given moment (or on many given moments), you will be driven – and excited – to succeed and to continue moving forward.

Why? Because your company will be more than just what you do, it will be based on *who you are*.

Can you learn to be successful? Yes. Passionate? No. But you can learn to uncover the passion that exists deep within you, just waiting to be unleashed. You can find and utilize the tools that you need (this book is one of them) to fan the fire and create unparalleled, lasting results for your business and in your life.

But you have to play an active role and you have to be engaged in the process. This is not a passive undertaking. Engagement leads to understanding and understanding leads to learning. Interest and enthusiasm are key factors to achieving understanding. They are also key factors in igniting entrepreneurial passion. When you want to learn, you will. Period.

And when you truly want to succeed, you are much more likely to. Why? Because you want it so much that you are willing to work for it and your passion drives you forward.

Understanding also creates confidence, an entrepreneur's most essential tool. Confidence makes success seem possible. Understanding puts it within reach.

Confidence comes from focusing on your Core Strengths from choosing a business idea that truly reflects who you are, what you are interested in, and what you are willing to devote your life to, gladly, and not just for the money or the fame – although we all know that having some of each is always a nice bonus.

Confidence is what makes it possible for entrepreneurs to take that leap, to leave their jobs and start their companies, to ask a bank or a relative for money, to talk wholesalers or vendors into taking a chance on their business, and to go knocking on doors looking for customers. This is what confident people do. They know that they are unlikely to get what they don't ask for and they are willing to do the asking. They know that if they stay true to their strengths and their mission and push forward, they will succeed.

And their confidence – and their enthusiasm – is contagious.

If you are reading this book, that entrepreneurial spirit is likely within you and just waiting to get out. Maybe you didn't run a lemonade stand or organize the neighbor kids into business ventures. Maybe you were the student, the parent or the co-worker who participated but didn't lead the way. Maybe you have been working at your corporate job for quite a few years and it is only just now starting to suffocate you. Maybe all you really need is a good dose of confidence to get started and on your entrepreneurial way – the confidence to step out there and focus on your true interests and strengths; the confidence, and the courage, to dare to achieve and succeed for you, *finally*.

Maybe you have plenty of confidence and the timing just hasn't been right until now. The Attraction Marketing strategies that I am going to introduce you to will help you get off to the fastest start possible as you undertake your entrepreneurial or other life-changing journey. Your time to *Be the Bulb!* has arrived.

Maybe you are an existing entrepreneur who is looking to grow your business. You may have made it past the survival stage but things just aren't moving as quickly as you'd like them to and your business isn't growing as strongly as you had originally planned. This book will teach you how to use Attraction Marketing to put the spotlight on you, your company and its products or services. You will learn how to focus on the energy that is inherent in strength-based branding to push your message out into the marketplace, where it will attract the customers that you need to grow your business. You will learn how to take your company to the next level, assuming that you made good decisions during its startup phase and it is on the right path. And if you didn't and it isn't? Here's your opportunity to get things back on the right track.

'Being true to myself and my Core Strengths sounds great,' you may be thinking, 'but I need to make money. I need to find customers who are willing to pay me for what I love to do, or make or sell. It is, after all, supposed to be a business. I have bills to pay, a family to support, things I want to buy and places I want to travel to. Isn't it asking too much to expect people to have the same interests that I do, and to be willing to give me their money for doing something that I love to do?'

No, it's not. Attraction Marketing will help you achieve all of these things, by focusing on your true strengths and interests, and by creating – and projecting – the passion that makes your offering very attractive to the right audience. Your commitment to your company, your expertise and your obvious engagement are all value-adding attributes. They reassure prospective customers that they are about to do business with a company that is truly interested in gaining, and keeping, their business.

The key is to identify and reach out to prospects who are ideally matched with your offering (which should be at the core of *any* target marketing effort, attraction-based or otherwise). Your ideal target customers will have many of the same interests and needs that led you to develop your business idea in the first place. At least they should, if your concept is built on an offering that is a true reflection of who you are and what you have to offer to the world. Is it a product that you needed and no one else offered? Is it a lifelong hobby that produces something of value to sell or share with others? Is it a service that is built on one of your true talents? There are potential customers in the marketplace who have similar interests and needs but different talents. They are looking to buy what they need, not create it. You must take the time to understand who these people (or businesses) are, and what they are looking for and why. You will never be able to find them otherwise.

In a later chapter, I am going to discuss the difference between benefits and attributes and their roles in message development. People make purchasing decisions for a variety of reasons, and often for less than obvious reasons. Understanding what they buy and why is critical to developing and promoting your offering. Directing your message and energies at prospects who are most likely to be interested in what you have to say and offer will be more efficient, and successful, than trying to broadcast your message – or your light – to the entire world. Traditional marketing calls this the difference between a rifle and a shotgun approach and that's a good metaphor for it. I also liken it to a 100-watt bulb glowing at full strength versus a dimmer-switched fixture set at only half light, The first attracts others to its light, to gather, to see detail, to read, to understand or to learn. The dimmed light provides enough light to see or set a mood, but not enough to work precisely. It is a background light that is present, but doesn't vie for our attention as strongly as a brighter, concentrated light will do in just about any setting. In your mind's eye, imagine spotlights and Klieg lights at an opening night event; lasers and fireworks in the night sky; headlights, roaring campfires and candles, or even a solitary candle that is burning in a darkened room.

Light. Attention. Focus. Power. We instinctively focus on light when it burns more brightly than the elements around it.

Be that bright, shining light. Identify your ideal customers and reach out to them by channeling your Motivational Energy to create and project a targeted, relevant message that speaks to your best prospects in a voice and tone that they understand and are attracted to. Shine brightly, not just in voice and message, but in everything that you do. Harness your Motivational Energy and put Attraction Marketing into practice to *Be the Bulb!* It is a life strategy as well as a business-building strategy. *Actually, it is a life-changing strategy.*

It is impossible to *Be the Bulb!* in just one area of your life. Once you ignite your passion, once you begin to project your light and set yourself apart from the crowd, once you begin to call attention to yourself, it will carry over into every part of your life. It has to. It is a light that you cannot hide or compartmentalize once it has begun to shine. Being true to your Core Strengths and interests will help bring every part of your life into balance. Your engagement will be real. Your confidence will grow. You will approach every part of your life in a more positive, focused and productive way. Attitude, as they say, is everything – and that will definitely be the case here – but it will be results that really make the difference. Attitude doesn't change things without effort. It is effort that produces results. Wishing and wanting will not get you what you want if you are not willing to work for it. Decide what you want, visualize the result, and then actively work toward it by creating opportunities to make success possible.

Attraction Marketing puts your light and energy in the path of people who can help you succeed. They will notice it, and you, and be drawn to your energy. And they will bring opportunities with them.

But only you can turn on the light. Only you can choose to make it happen.

Choose to be the bright, positive light that others are drawn to. Be the person who people think of as dynamic, energetic or even brilliant. Choose to interact with positive, energetic people. Make it easy for them to be drawn to your light and to help it burn brighter. Choose to be successful in what you choose to do. Choose to release the brilliance within you and let your light shine through. Choose to light up every room that you enter, and to bring new energy to every project that you join in.

Choose to *Be the Bulb!*

Success Is Not Accidental

Learn to *Be the Bulb!* and to shine brightly, in business and life. Put the spotlight on your best strengths and interests, and on the best benefits that your products and services have to offer. Make your company a standout and you will find people standing in line to do business with you. Learn how to make waves when you enter a room or set the business world on fire with your energy. I'm about to show you how to make it all happen.

Let me plant this thought in your mind before we begin in earnest: *Success is not accidental.* You have to work at it. But once you understand what it takes to attract and facilitate success – how to be successful – you can create success over and over again.

A while back, I presented a workshop on online branding and social marketing at an event which also featured GoDaddy.com CEO and Founder Bob Parsons as its keynote speaker. Bob told the group that he disagreed with my statement that 'success is not accidental'. According to Bob, luck and perspective had more to do with his own success – something along the lines of being in the right place at the right time and being smart (Bob would say lucky) enough to recognize the opportunity that those circumstances presented. I'd argue that Bob's entrepreneurial instincts had as much to do with his extraordinary success as anything else. Bob understands what it takes to *create opportunities* to be successful. His Sixteen Rules for Success are a testimonial to that. (You can read them online at www.bobparsons.com.) Creating opportunity is one thing. Making the most of those opportunities (and others that come your way) is quite another. Bob is a master at capitalizing on opportunity. The most successful entrepreneurs always are.

Success is *not* accidental. You have to work at it. I'm one of those people who firmly believes that success has a lot less to do with luck than with circumstance. If we create the right set of circumstances and then place ourselves and our well-thought-out plans within them, we can and we will encourage opportunities to be successful and we can, and we will, achieve our goals. That 'right' set of circumstances includes knowing what we are good at, knowing what we are capable of, knowing how to channel and target that energy toward our goals, and being willing to do the work that all of this really requires. It means being open to opportunity – whether we create it, invite it or stumble upon it – and being ready to make the most of the opportunities that come our way. It means understanding how important passion is to making our dreams possible, learning how to engage, ignite and continually fuel that passion, and possessing the confidence that it takes to make the leap – to start a business, a venture or a new relationship – and then stick with it until it begins to turn the corner and take on a life of its own.

And yes, it does take a little luck, and I'll grant Bob the perspective part as well. There are no guarantees in the business world or in life in general. We surely learn that as we move through life. But here is something that you can count on: Once you have learned what it takes to be successful and you have used that knowledge to create your first success, you will be relieved of a very large burden. *The fear of failure will have been eliminated from your life.* Once you understand what it takes to be successful and have proven to yourself that you CAN create success and that you CAN be successful, you will realize that you now also have the power to RE-CREATE that success, even if it is in another shape or form, in another location or under an entirely different set of circumstances. You will realize that you have the ability to create your own set of circumstances that facilitate success, to make the most of any opportunities that come your way and to create your own opportunities for success when the universe does not seem to be providing them quickly enough on its own.

Talk about empowerment!

The power of that knowledge will energize you and it will make your Bulb shine even brighter. The stronger your light becomes, the greater your success will be. You can ignite that light, nurture it, project it, protect it and build it, beginning today. I'm about to show you how.

We're going to begin with some basic business and branding concepts that will help you understand just how powerful a role Motivational Energy and Attraction Marketing can play in every part of your life. You don't have to be an aspiring entrepreneur or a business owner to benefit from these concepts. Read the sections on personal branding and relationship building and you'll realize that everything that I present can be put to work in every part of your life. The first part of this book focuses on how you can *Be the Bulb!* and attract more of what you are looking for out of life, including the types of people you need to nurture, encourage, support and applaud you. The second half explains how to put the power of Attraction Marketing to work to shine the spotlight on you, your company and its products and services. Read them both and your personal and professional light is sure to be magnified.

Let's get started by doing a little groundwork.

Be The Bulb!

Part I: Laying the Groundwork

Chapter 1
Be the Bulb, Be the Brand

We are exposed to thousands of brands every day. They invade our lives and influence the choices that we make. People seek out and pay more for strong and trusted brands. They compare brands, wear brands, eat brands and buy brands. Human beings are brand conscious to a fault. We consider those who aren't to be 'different', and maybe just a little too organic. Remember the failure of generic brands in the 1980's? I rest my case. Today, even environmentally-conscious products are branded (and command a premium!) and 'green' marketing is a hugely growing industry. People like to be green, and to be 'seen being green'. Saving the world has become a status symbol.

A brand is a relationship based on perception. It represents the sum total of the feelings that an individual has about a product or a company. Think about what you are wearing, what you drive, what's in your pantry at home and why you chose those brands versus others. Your purchases were based on information, experience and perception. You made a comparison – and a decision – either consciously or subconsciously.

Brands also apply to individuals, both personally and professionally. Everyone has a personal brand, whether they realize it – or work at it –or not. Your personal brand is a perception or emotion, held by someone other than you, that describes their experience of relating with you. Your brand is a reflection of who you are, what you do and how well you do it. It is the energy that tells the world who you are and what you have to offer.

Your personal brand is the information that surrounds you, and it includes your reputation, your resume and your Google results. It is the way you carry and conduct yourself on a daily basis, and how you interact with people who know you — and especially with those who don't. It is the level and the quality of the work that you are known for, how visible you are in the marketplace and the company that you keep, both on the job and off.

If someone has never met or worked with you, their perception of you may be based on what they have read, seen or heard about you. This includes what others have said (or whispered), written or blogged about you. Their perceptions may be an accurate assessment of you or a total misperception. They are perceptions that you can actively work to reinforce or labor to erase. In no case can you choose to ignore them.

Everything about you is part of your brand. It is the word of mouth that circulates about you, the press you receive and the buzz that all of that creates. It is the clothes you wear, the strength of your handshake, and the way that you enter a room, pose a question, listen to the answer, speak to others and present your ideas. It is your knowledge of your industry and your ability to talk about it, your attitude, your personality, your approachability and your promptness. All of these are cues that send signals to others about you and all of them are part of the persona that is your personal brand.

Everyone has a personal brand and everyone needs a personal brand, whether you are an entrepreneur or an employee, a CEO or a clerk, in a blue collar or a white collar profession, or focused on building your professional or your personal relationships (or both!). A personal brand can and will help you get what you want and need from life. It is your most potent attraction tool.

You are what you put out into the marketplace. You can choose to be a brilliant, unique brand or you can be the bland, un-marketed, lower-price brand that no one values. You can be the strong brand or the weak brand. You can choose to be a market leader or a me-too brand. You can choose to be a stand out or just another brand in the crowd. Choose to be a standout. Choose to be noticed, recognized, appreciated and valued. Choose to be a strong and confident brand that reflects the real you. The light created by that reflection will help you attract the people and opportunities that you need in your life. True light creates true opportunity. Be a beacon for success.

Be the Bulb!

These days, it is likely that more people will meet you online for the first time than by shaking your hand in person. They may have heard about you from others or read about you in the press. Many will go looking for information on you and your business on their own, without contacting you or your company. Some will be potential customers – people who are thinking about doing business with you, but are looking to learn more about who you are and what you have to offer. They can find out pretty much everything that they want to know about you and your company by investing some dedicated research time online. They can talk to your current and former customers, learn about your contacts and your network, read reviews about your products and the quality of your service, and perhaps even learn what you did when you went out last night. Much of this information is always just a few clicks away. *Never, ever forget this.*

People are gathering data and opinions and forming perceptions about you or your business without seeking — or getting — any direct input or interaction from you. They are working with what is already out there, in the marketplace, whether you intentionally placed it there or not. If you are not actively working to develop, maintain and promote a positive personal brand in the marketplace, you are ignoring your most powerful marketing tool: You. If you are not actively working to create, promote and protect your personal brand, you are leaving one of your most valuable assets to chance: You. If you are not creating and cultivating your personal brand, others will do it for you, sometimes with malice. Are you willing to leave your brand, your personal and your professional reputation, in the hands of the marketplace? Are you willing to passively accept the reputation cards that you are dealt or are you willing to actively work to build them into a better hand?

Do not let random chance define your personal identity or your brand, online or off. An important part of *Being the Bulb!* is Being the Brand. You must take action to ensure that others see you in the accurate and positive way that you want to be perceived.

These same rules apply to your company and its products and services. If you are a business owner, your personal brand will also be colored by your company's reputation, the way you service your accounts, the quality and behavior of the employees who work for you and, again, by how visible you are in the marketplace. If you are a visible business owner, your company's reputation will be impacted by the quality of your reputation. Work to protect both of them. They are inseparable.

Our personal brands are more important than ever in this age of personal search engines and social networks, where we 'Google' people we want to know, date or do business with. They are especially important to professionals and business owners whose companies deal in services. When you sell an intangible product — a service — your reputation and the reputation of your company are your most valuable assets. Positive comments and referrals by clients, friends, associates, peers and former customers are critical to new business development. Even referral customers are likely to search for more information in the marketplace. That's why reputation management is so important. The quality of your search engine results can play a big role in your professional success. The first few pages of your results must convey the types of positive links and information that you want prospective customers to see.

A strong personal brand also sets you apart from the competition. A well-developed, positive brand that is actively projected and promoted in the marketplace will call attention to you and your company in a beneficial way. It will help you as you network for new contacts and customers (people will have already heard of you!), shop for financing or business services, and help you attract opportunities to grow your business in new and exciting ways. Be the Brand and you are well on your way to *Being the Bulb!*

In this day and age when we are all deluged by emails, how do we decide whose email to open first when time is limited? At a time when anyone can have a website — *and everyone does* – how do we decide which websites are worth visiting when we see them posted in email addresses or in solicitations that come our way? We decide partially on the strength of the headline but mostly on the strength of the sender. We decide whether or not to open it, visit it or read it based on the perceptions we have about the person or company who initiated the contact. This is branding at work. Period. Your name (or your company's or product's name) should set the stage and with a positive perception that creates interest, so that the recipient wants to open your email, wants to visit your website, wants to go to your store or otherwise act in the way that you'd like them to. You want your name — which is the most inescapable element of your personal brand — to become firmly associated with 'what you are known for'. Ideally, this should reflect a set of positive values and attributes that translate to benefits — benefits that make you desirable to the types of people whom you wish to attract. I call it 'claiming a piece of marketspace in the prospect's mind'. It is fundamental product positioning — Branding 101 — and it applies to you, your company and its products.

In the world of marketing, there are four steps that must typically take place for a message to be considered successful. First, you must get the Attention of the recipient. Then, you must incite their Interest in some way. Hopefully, that interest will create a Desire within the prospect to take the final step, which is Action. Action can be visiting the website, spreading the word, using a coupon, buying a product, or becoming a repeat customer. Whatever your objective, the steps are always the same — and they always begin in the same manner: *you must attract your target's attention and capture their interest if you want to be heard.* Desire must be preceded by Interest and Interest will not develop without Attention. There are many ways to attract Attention, but it will be your brand and the set of perceptions that it creates that will impact Interest the most.

What can you do to ensure that your name is associated with a strong and positive brand? First, you must understand the elements of effective branding. A strong brand is clear, concise and built on value-adding benefits. When you hear its name, your name, there is no mistaking the connotation. Strong brands don't 'hem and haw'. They are based on a clear, easy to understand message and everything about them — their look, their feel and their tone — supports and conveys that message.

Brands can be products, services, companies, people or even places that have recognizable and consistently marketed traits and characteristics. When a company creates a brand, it is creating a promise. It is creating an image and identity that promises to fulfill a need of some kind. That promise also creates a set of expectations for how the brand will perform. Successful brands deliver as promised. Always. They consistently meet the expectations that they have created. They have to. In this age of social networking, blogs and YouTube, you can not fool anyone for very long.

Personal branding takes that concept and applies it to people. When we create a personal brand for ourselves, we must focus on our existing Core Strengths and capabilities – *strengths and capabilities that we already possess* – and present them to the world in a consistent way that both creates and fulfills our 'brand promise'. That promise should build on our *existing and real strengths, talents and capabilities* – which is an important part of the equation. Strong brands are authentic and genuine. Their promise is driven by their inherent features and strengths.

There's a critical difference between product brands and personal brands. Product brands are *designed and created* to fulfill a specific set of needs. People are not. Corporate or product brands build desirable features and attributes into the brand at conception, often based on a carefully outlined branding strategy. (In other words, the strategy precedes the product.) People are born as unique individuals, each with our own mix of strengths and weaknesses. We are not created to a pre-conceived set of specifications. There's a lot of genetic and environmental roulette involved, regardless of who our parents or our ancestors may be.

Personal branding is not about becoming who you think you *should be*. It's not about creating a 'brand new' you. It's about letting your true strengths, talents and values shine through. It is about using and 'packaging' the strengths that you already possess and creating a 'brand promise' that is based on your talents and values. It is about becoming the best possible, already-existing you, and then presenting that authentic (but polished) brand to the world.

A strong brand is consistent. It is always presented in an environment that is consistent with its message and in a way that supports its message. That consistency and familiarity creates trust. Potential customers know what to expect from the brand (whether a person or product) and feel relatively confident that their experience with it will be similar with each interaction. Trust is a powerful motivator. Consumers buy brands that they know and trust.

A strong brand makes a statement that positions its subject firmly in a target's mind. It is based on a relevant benefit promise and a compelling Reason Why. That promise and Reason Why are the tools that will help you claim a piece of real estate, or marketspace, in the prospect's mind. In marketing-speak, we call this concept 'positioning', a term that was popularized by Jack Trout and Al Ries in series of articles in *Advertising Age* in the early 1970's and explained in depth in their 1981 book, *Positioning* (which was updated and re-released as a 20th anniversary edition in 2000). A positioning statement outlines what you or your product has to offer to prospects in a way that they can relate to, understand and embrace. A positioning statement defines and claims a meaningful piece of marketspace for your brand. It is a statement of promise to fulfill a need or desire that is important to your target audience. Importance creates relevance. Relevance captures Attention and creates Interest. Interest leads to Desire and then to Action. Strong brands are built on a clear positioning statement and strategy.

A strong brand focuses on the customer, not the product. Its promise (message) speaks to the target audience in familiar language and in an environment in which they are comfortable. It focuses on the benefit that the brand promises to provide and includes reasons why the brand will actually perform as promised.

It is important to understand the difference between Benefits and Attributes. Attributes are features or characteristics of a product. A benefit is the utility or advantage that an attribute provides. It is the promised result. Consumers rarely buy products for their features. (Oh, they may say that they do and they may spend endless hours comparing features and attributes — think cup holder configurations, reclining seats and DVD screens on different car models — but the actual purchase decision is typically made for far less obvious reasons.) They typically buy a product (or service) for the benefit (or bundle of benefits) that its tangible or intangible features provide.

Let's use a Burberry branded raincoat as an example. Its attributes (features) include its being well-made, water-repellant and warm, with secure pockets, classic styling and trademark plaid accents. It is also typically offered at a premium price point in upscale clothing stores. In the case of the Burberry raincoat, status is the benefit that many of its buyers derive. The plaid lining and other trademark features make it possible for others to easily identify the brand of the coat when the buyer wears it. The buyer could have purchased another (less expensive) brand of raincoat to perform the basic function of staying dry, but chose a brand and style that also satisfied other, higher-level needs. Status may be an intangible benefit, but it is a very strong motivator.

Humans are motivated by many different needs. Some are very basic, others are much more complex. In his 1943 paper, A *Theory of Human Motivation*, Abraham Maslow identified a hierarchy of five core physiological and psychological needs that drive most human behavior and are the foundation of individual personality. The five levels include Physiological needs such as eating, drinking, sleeping and warmth; needs for Safety, including personal and financial security, health and well-being; a need for both non-sexual and sexual Love and Belonging such as family, friendship and intimacy; needs for Esteem and self-respect; and needs for Self Actualization or Growth, which are at the highest level of Maslow's hierarchy. According to Maslow, Self-Actualization includes the need to explore, discover and learn, and strive to realize our full potential as individuals. These needs are enduring and continue throughout our lives, even after other lower-level needs have been met.

In the case of the raincoat, we could argue that buying a Burberry satisfies needs for status and self-esteem. Buyers want others to know that they are successful enough to be able to afford the garment over a lesser brand, that they are concerned with style and that they are savvy enough to recognize a good value, which a Burberry coat is branded to convey, despite its price. In fact, marketing — including price, promotion and distribution — all worked together to create this brand perception. Burberry raincoats are expensive and they are not available for sale just anywhere. The Burberry folks have created a very strong brand that has universal connotations for many. Not into Burberry? Insert any high-status, typically high-priced brand in this example instead. Designer clothes, as an entire category, would fit into this example just as well. They do not keep you warmer, nor are they any more useful than any other brand of clothing but, for some consumers, they do satisfy Love and Belonging and Self-Esteem needs.

Here's the point: You have to know who your target audience is and understand *why* they buy in order to craft a compelling benefit-driven positioning strategy. Understand their needs, know their desires, and create a statement that conveys how your product will specifically fulfill that demand.

In the case of personal branding, that product is YOU. Strength-based branding utilizes the unique combination of you (or your product's) inherent strengths to create a compelling and valuable benefit to the people whom you seek to bring into your life, either as customers or as individuals who can create and facilitate opportunities for you. Because your benefit statement is based on your inherent strengths, and the genuine benefit and value that those strengths offer, it is completely authentic and very magnetic.

It is this focus on strength-based branding that is at the core of *Being the Bulb!* Here's why:

When you focus on your genuine, inherent strengths, when you put your authentic best foot forward based on what you are interested in, what you are good at and what you love to do, you create a true, strong light that can't help but shine through. Remember that passion we talked about? This is it. This is you. When your passion shines through, interacting with others becomes more about sharing than selling, and more about connecting than making contact. People who are tuned into that same frequency will be drawn to you, your energy and your message. They will want to be near you. They will want to be part of your world.

This is the foundation of a true, benefit-driven, value-adding branding strategy. Your inner passion, energy and strengths are at the core of who you are (and who you can become) as an evolved individual and a successful entrepreneur. When you actively project that energy into the world and the greater marketplace, through actions, words and images (and yes, word of mouth), your true, positive energy will attract like-minded people to you and your offering. When you are doing what you love — and doing it well — the world will be interested and the world will find its way to your front door. Focusing on your Core Strengths builds your confidence. Period. *It has to. You are doing what you love to do!* As your confidence builds, your light grows stronger and your energy fuels itself. You light up, you project, you attract who and what you need, your success builds your confidence and the entire cycle repeats itself and feeds your energy.

If you have done the work to target that energy and direct it toward the appropriate audiences — to put it in the path of the people who can help you succeed – they will be drawn to you and you *will* make progress towards your goals. You will attract what you want and need from life. You will be successful. You will achieve all of this and more if you choose to Be the Brand and *Be the Bulb!*

Start thinking about what you are interested in and excited about. Start thinking about your strengths and your talents. Start thinking about what you do or have to offer to others that would add value to their lives and to the world at large. Start thinking about who you are and what you want to be known for from this point forward. *Then act that way, starting today.* Start thinking about why and how you want to become well-respected, well-loved, successful and sought after because all of that is about to happen.

Now let's start talking about *how*.

Chapter 2
Understanding Attraction Marketing

Believe in yourself and the world will agree. Project confidence and the world will have confidence in you. When you choose to *Be the Bulb!* and project positive, magnetic energy, the world will be attracted to what you have to offer. I have been doing this successfully for more than 20 years and I am here to tell you that it works. I can turn up the light when I am feeling ambitious and looking for new opportunities, or I can dial it down when I want to go 'under cover' for a while (though, with time, that becomes increasingly hard to do, and especially in these days of long Google trails).

Why does it work? People who love what they do are excited and confident. We can't help but give off positive energy when we are doing our thing and spending time within our realms. We approach life with enthusiasm and zest and look forward to the dawning of each new day (well, maybe not the dawning ...). We have a spring in our step because we are happy about where we are going. We smile as we move from one task to another because we understand how those pieces make up the whole and how, together, they all keep us moving forward.

We are happy, and it shows, in just about everything that we do. It shows in the way that we approach life and the people who are part of our lives on any given day, and in the quality, and the depth, of our work.

Our Core Strengths represent our 'best stuff'. When we focus on them, we can't help but put our best foot forward and our shiny sides out. But happy feet and shiny faces are not enough. Strong personal brands are built on saying *and* doing. A brand is more than an image and an offer or a bundle of benefits. It has to live up to and fulfill its promise. *It has to deliver.* If we tell the world that we are good at something, we have to be good at it. We have to deliver on our promise. We have to *Be the Bulb!* first, to get on the radar and to get their Attention and Interest, and then we have to Be the Brand to encourage Desire, Action and — here's a new one —

Commitment. Strength-based branding takes what we are good at, what we have a passion for, and puts it out there for others to find and be attracted to. It must be based on true light that come from true strengths — Core Strengths — so that it remains strong and true throughout the interaction. Performing as expected and promised (a successful interaction) builds relationships and relationships provide opportunities to grow and succeed, both personally and professionally.

A personal branding statement is similar to a mission statement. It is a summary of what you do on a daily basis to get to who you want to be and become. And because a personal branding statement is based on your true Core Strengths, it should be intuitive and easy to live by. Strength-based personal branding is authentic personal branding. It represents the Real You. It should be easy to live up to the image, the actions, the purpose and the quality of the work that you are offering because the promise that is made (your brand promise) is a *true reflection of your strengths and interests.*

Branding works the same way with products. A product is created for a reason. There is a problem to solve, a need to fulfill or a task to perform. The most successful products are created to fulfill an un-met or un-served need in the marketplace. They have a purpose. Focusing on that purpose and strength is authentic marketing. Sometimes, as I discussed earlier, the benefit that is derived from buying or using a product may not be apparent or obvious. It may, for example, be status, convenience or affirmation of some type (all of which are intangible benefits) versus better mileage, cleaner clothes or fewer calories (which provide measurable, discernible differences). Attraction Marketing digs down to the core benefits, the Core Strengths, of the product and focuses on them. It puts those strengths front and center and projects their energy at high potential target prospects. These are people who have a related need or desire and are attracted to that bundle of benefits and, by association, the product (brand). They are pulled in and often bring others with them. And, if the product is authentic and it lives up to its promise, then there will also be word of mouth and good buzz – elements of viral marketing that will fuel the brand's energy and attract even greater numbers of customers.

Understanding Attraction Marketing

Attraction Marketing is strength-based branding and a true PULL marketing strategy that works for both people and products. *Being the Bulb* means broadcasting a light and energy that is True, Strong, Authentic and Consistent. It means marketing that brand and image in a way that is similarly True, Strong, Authentic, Consistent and Targeted at the people, opportunities and events that fit it best. A true, strong brand that is marketed with a clear message and targeted at its highest potential customers will succeed. Its energy will grow and the brand will get stronger. Strong brands are Bulbs; bright, shiny bulbs. Weak, inconsistent or poorly communicated brands are not.

A brand needs to shine brightly. *Always.*

I need to bring in some traditional marketing concepts now to demonstrate how powerful Attraction Marketing can be – and to show how it is changing the way that we think of conventional marketing terms.

I used a term a few paragraphs ago: PULL strategy. The debate over the merits of a PUSH versus a PULL strategy has been going back and forth for decades (I had to say that. Pun intended.)

Traditional marketing defined a PULL strategy as one designed to encourage end consumers to want a product so much that they PULL it through the distribution channel (for example, by buying it or by asking for it at the store if they don't find it on the shelves). A PUSH strategy was traditionally aimed at other channel members (such as distributors and store owners) in an attempt to persuade them to stock and promote specific products. (The core points of this definition are courtesy of the American Marketing Association, a long-time standard setter and educator in the advertising and market industry.)

As with much of our lives and especially in the business world, the Internet has changed the way in which we approach the four P's of advertising strategy: price, product, promotion and place (distribution) – including how PUSH and PULL marketing strategies are utilized.

In today's Internet-driven world, we PUSH our information out into the marketplace to make ourselves visible and, hopefully, get found. Potential customers PULL what they want from us, absorb it and then also spread it around. PUSHing and PULLing occur simultaneously and repeatedly, in a process that I call 'churning'. Information goes out, gets pulled in and then is passed around to others. Advertising and marketing communications — and, in fact, information of all types — are part of a continual flow that knows no limits or boundaries. Even to call it a two-way street would be limiting.

A PUSH strategy requires Active Attention by the marketer. (We are going to learn about Active Attention in Chapter 3.) A focused, active effort is required to put information and energy out into the marketplace where it can be seen and found. Being Visible is at the core of a modern PUSH strategy.

Today, manufacturers PUSH information on their products and how to purchase them out into the marketplace via websites and online information exchange networks. Sometimes this is in addition to physical 'brick and mortar' stores. Often it is instead of them. Traditional advertising and selling methods still exist, but they have evolved to become much more selective than they used to be as prospect audiences have become much more fragmented by an ever-increasing universe of media and communication choices.

The Internet has changed the way that people obtain, process and use information. Today, we go online to get news, to learn, to communicate with clients, friends and family, to make purchases, to sell items, to share information and to build our social and professional networks. This is only a small sampling of what we can achieve online. The list goes on and on.

We use search engines to sort through huge, seemingly unlimited amounts of information to find what we are looking for and to make it all digestible. When we find something of interest, a website perhaps, we PULL what we want from it, either in information, products, contacts or additional links. This act of PULLing information from the Internet (or the Sunday paper or whatever medium you may be using) requires Active Attention on your part. *You are actively seeking out information with purpose.* Often, when you find what you have been looking for — or even a totally unrelated but very interesting or funny tidbit – you SHARE it with others: your friends, your family, your network, and your contacts.

Understanding Attraction Marketing

Today, prospects use the Internet to look for information, compare products and sources and then either identify a physical store location to visit or continue to complete their purchase online. Today's PULL strategy encourages prospects to find and pull information to themselves online and then make and share their research, buying choices and experiences with others. The entire process often takes place entirely online, without any interaction from a salesperson. Few or no physical trips to the store may be involved. Users may also push information around, adding to it as it moves through the marketplace. Sellers must make sure that accurate, positive information is readily available on their company, its products and their benefits. (This can be challenging for marketers who find that they must not only PUSH good information out into the marketplace but also MONITOR it on an ongoing basis to ensure that it remains positive.)

Being Visible and Accessible online has never been more important. Why? Because in today's marketplace, companies aren't finding customers anymore, prospective customers are finding companies. Prospects search for information with purpose and then PULL what they need and want toward themselves, where they may then choose to also SHARE it with others. Marketers have to Be Visible so that they can Get Found by prospects. This is how today's global marketplace works. You must make it easy for your customers to find you, your company and the products or information that they seek, online or off and on demand, 24 hours a day, seven days a week. No holidays. No weekends. No excuses.

This is also how Attraction Marketing works. When we focus on our Core Strengths, target our offering at a specific audience and actively PUSH our energy and message into the marketplace, it makes it possible for us to be noticed and Get Found. When we shine brightly, we attract others with our light. People whose needs and interests are relevant to the message and energy that we are projecting will be attracted to who we are and what we have to offer and they will PULL themselves closer to see what we (or our products) are all about. If our light (promise) feels true and strong, they will be drawn even closer to our confidence, our power and our light. When we PUSH our energy outward to PULL others in closer, we are *Being the Bulb!* Attraction Marketing is the concept that explains how this process works

— and it goes far beyond traditional PUSH or PULL definitions, or most basic marketing concepts for that matter.

Attraction Marketing draws a lot of its effectiveness from target marketing, which is a fundamental marketing strategy. The smaller and better defined a target audience is, the more efficient the marketing effort to that audience will be. In marketing, targeting is often compared to a rifle versus shotgun approach. A rifle is always going to be more precise and efficient. You can better channel your energy to focus on the target, instead of having to spread your light all over the place. (Think of the difference between a spotlight or a focused work light versus a general, overhead light. Which provides greater clarity and detail?) You can fine tune the message and make it highly relevant, instead of opting for a broader appeal that casts a wider net and doesn't really hit home with anyone. You can ask direct questions, out loud, and you can put people who look and sound like your target into your advertising without worrying about excluding potential sales prospects.

Targeting takes the message and makes it personal. You are not really communicating with someone unless you speak (or write or broadcast) to them in a way which is relevant and meaningful — especially in today's crowded media and messaging marketplaces. You are not really communicating unless your intended audience notices you and hears you. You are not really communicating unless the people whom you are reaching out to acknowledge that reach and pay attention to what you are saying to them.

Think of it as talking with someone, and not just at them. You are not really communicating unless your message is both received and absorbed.

When you know exactly who you want to talk to or sell to and what you want to say to them, you can channel your message in a highly targeted direction and take aim at your target. You can actively and purposely work to put information not just 'out there', but directly in their path, where they can see it, even trip over it, time and time again. Target marketing to small groups will make it possible for you to look like you are everywhere, when in fact you may in the same place, in front of your best prospects, over and over again. It will look like you are everywhere because you will be everywhere in *their* world.

A PUSH strategy is very important in both Attraction Marketing and target marketing. As with most things in life, it's a matter of pushing smarter, not just harder, and in a well-defined direction. Here's a visual example: Think of it as pushing a shopping cart up a sidewalk on a hill (a directed and focused task, with parameters and a path) versus herding a flock of sheep randomly up that same hill. Anyone or anything that is also on that sidewalk (with its defined parameters) is bound to come across your path (and vice versa). With the sheep, it's a crap shoot at best. They may meet you, or a single sheep, or they may go down the hill using a different path entirely to avoid you. You may never meet them and they may never meet you. It's hardly an efficient scenario. And those people you meet by taking the sidewalk? They will tend to be people of a similar mindset, with similar interests and habits. (They chose the sidewalk also!) These are the people whom you will be most successful speaking with.

Here's another point to keep in mind: PUSHing only works to a certain point. Once you have the attention of your target, you need to generate enough light and put enough energy into projecting that light to stay on their radar and in their world, without overpowering them. You need to Be Visible and Get Found, but once you are found, you need to let the PULLing begin. Be visible, be accessible, be true and be strong, but do not push too hard and overpower your audience or try to wear them down into taking action. If you push too hard they will tune you out or even block you or avoid you (which is not the action that you want them to take). It's a fine line to walk and successful brand managers know intuitively how and when to modulate their energy, their light, their advertising, their voice and their brightness to achieve the best results.

In Attraction Marketing, we put our energy into the marketplace in a way which attracts back the types of people and opportunities that we need in our lives to be successful. You must PUSH (project) positive information on yourself, your company and its products in order to Be Found by and Attract people who will become your customers, mentors, suppliers, partners, advocates or even soulmates. Whom you attract will be determined by the message and energy that you project. The truer you are to your Core Strengths, the truer your message and your energy will be and the more relevant, productive and potentially helpful the people who are attracted to you, through your energy and message, will be. The process begins by actively working to put your message and energy in front of the people whom you want to do business with. These steps are called Channeling and Active Attention. You then 'flip the switch' and actively apply effort and energy to send your message out to the world, where it can be seen and be found. The more energy that you apply, the more Visible you and your message will be. The truer that you stay to your message, the stronger and clearer your energy, your message and your BRAND will be. The more ways that you find to broadcast and strengthen your message by building on your Core Strengths, the stronger your power to attract others will be. People are attracted to positive energy. When they find it, see it, or find themselves near it, they want to get closer. They want to be in its light and feel the energy. They will PULL themselves in and often bring others with them. Fueled by the new energy and attention, the light will grow even stronger. It will become even more visible and will attract even greater numbers to its energy.

Attraction Marketing is a true PUSH-PULL strategy. You want your actions to cause a definite reaction. You want the projection of your energy to pull others into your sphere. It requires Active Attention and effort. Wishing and wanting alone are not going to cut it. Why? Because, outside of nature, very few things happen on their own. If you want something, you have to ask for it, go get it or work for it. You have to be actively involved in the process in some way, even if it is only to recognize and act on the opportunities that come your way. Napoleon Hill said it best: 'Riches do not respond to wishes. They respond to definite plans backed by definite desires, through constant persistence.' You have to take action. You have to put energy into the marketplace so that it can bring energy — and opportunities — back, whether as sales, repeat sales, referrals, acclaim, or whatever you happen to be in need of.

You have to *Be the Bulb!* and be invested in the process in order to realize a return on your investment. Wishing and wanting without work is not going to get you anywhere.

Understanding Attraction Marketing

Attraction Marketing is a strategy that works whether you are marketing people or products. It takes the best of both PUSH and PULL strategies and teams them up with targeted, highly focused communication to build and promote a successful brand. It is a strategy for authentic living, messaging and branding and it is the true definition of marketing in today's ever-expanding marketplace. Attraction Marketing explains how, like a magnet, you can use channeled, focused energy and a PUSH/PULL strategy to create dynamic relationships that result in movement, action, sales and success.

Can you see the enormous potential? Are you beginning to understand just how powerful it can be to put the principles of Attraction Marketing to work and *Be the Bulb?* The excitement that you're beginning to feel is a proverbial 'light bulb over your head', Eureka! type of moment. As you start to realize what is possible, your own energy will begin to build. As you start working your way through the process, your enthusiasm, your energy and your confidence will take off. In many ways, it is a self-fulfilling process. If you do the work and follow the process, you will attract opportunity and make progress towards your goals. You will be fueling, and assuring, your own success, every step of the way. The word 'empowering' has never been used in a more appropriate context.

Being the Bulb is about putting your Core Strengths front and center and projecting the positive energy that they create. It is about shining brightly in order to attract the types of people, opportunities and events that you want and need in your life to become (and be) a successful entrepreneur. It is based on the concept of Motivational Energy, which works for people, products and companies. You can put it to work for you starting today. Let's find out how.

Be The Bulb!

Chapter 3
Motivational Energy Explained

What makes some people dynamic? What fills them with energy and contagious enthusiasm? It is the Motivational Energy that exists within them: internal, combustible energy that creates the dynamo that drives them, and makes them a dynamic speaker, a dynamic employee and a dynamic entrepreneur or business partner.

Motivational Energy is the product of the passion and purpose that comes from truly believing in — and wanting — something and then actively going after it. It is most powerful when it is highly authentic, meaning that it is based on a person or a product's Core Strengths. It is most effective when it is directed toward a specific goal, and it is highly contagious when it is effectively captured, channeled and projected outward.

Motivational Energy has very little to do with charisma or charm, although the people that we are often drawn to tend to have generous helpings of both. Motivational Energy comes from within. It draws its strength from what is already present. It is not a facade or a 'face' that can be publicly put on. It is a naturally occurring output that is created when we focus on our true strengths, talents and interests. It is the synergy that is created when we focus on a product's true benefits. Motivational Energy can not be artificially created, but it can — and it should — be nurtured, encouraged and controlled.

When we focus on our true strengths and talents, we project a positive self image and energy that conveys confidence and attracts people in search of those qualities. Conversely, if we project negative energy (or a false front), we will tend to attract negative energy, events and people. The signals that we send out are like magnets that attract a similar type of energy. Regardless of what you have heard about how opposites attract, *like tends to attract like* in most cases.

Motivational Energy includes an *active* element. Creating it requires your active participation, your energy and your effort. *You must know what you want, know what you have to work with and then play an active role in creating your success.* If you are looking to sit back and just let things happen, this is not the book for you.

Generating Motivational Energy is not a passive, wishful process. The marketplace cannot see what is within you. It cannot see your intentions. The marketplace — and the people within it — can only see what you 'put out there'. They can only see your actions and the energy that you project. Action is required to facilitate the process, to PUSH and project, to create the light that leads to Visibility, and to generate the energy that leads to being Found. Action and attention are what create momentum and turn desire and intentions into reality. Together they create the movement that is needed to get anyone, or anything, from Point A to Point B.

Motivational Energy requires ACTIVE ATTENTION. Yes, you have to want it, but you can't just will it to happen. You have to go out and get what you want. You have to actively put the mechanisms in place that attract what you want to come to you. You have to find and fuel the Motivational Energy that is already inside of you and you must channel that energy to attract what you want in your life. You have to choose to shine brightly and to create your own success. You have to choose to *Be the Bulb!*

Where the Power Comes From

The power you need to succeed exists inside of you. You have the ability to draw from it, build on it and channel it in productive ways that move you closer to your goals. Motivational Energy is empowering, in the most primal, basic way. *You can do this.*

A simple formula explains how Motivational Energy is created within us: $M/E = MC^2$. Motivational Energy (M/E) is created when MC (= My Core Strengths) are identified and amplified (= squared). When we focus on an inherent strength and magnify it, its potential to help us achieve our goals grows exponentially. This is especially true if the strength, talent or passion that we choose to focus on has lain dormant until this time because it was unrecognized or underutilized.

Your Core Strengths are what you bring to the table. They represent the Core of You: the strengths, talents, passions and leanings that are inherent to who you are and have always been. They are an important part of what you have to offer as a person, in both your personal and professional relationships. They are part of the tool box that you will carry with you throughout your life, whether you choose to draw from it or not. They play a big part in what you, as an employee, a manager, a consultant or a volunteer have to offer to the organizations that you choose to work with. They are the essence of what you bring to all of your relationships, whether they are professional or highly personal.

A Core Strength is something that you have always had an interest in, or been naturally 'good at'. It is some skill that comes easier to you than another. It is a topic that always holds your interest when others can't. Core Strengths include interests and passions as well as skills and talents. You do not choose a Core Strength. It chooses you. You are born with it. You can develop it, or build on it, but you cannot create it from scratch. It is inherent to who you are.

Core Strengths reflect Who You Are, not Who You Would Like To Be. This isn't about 'Brand New Me', this is about building and projecting a strength-based, authentically focused organic Brand Me. When you focus on your Core Strengths, when you build a business or pursue a passion that is based on a Core Strength, you are not becoming someone or something else, you are building on You. You are putting your best, most genuine foot forward and stepping with purpose. You are letting your true Bulb shine Brightly. Creating and projecting Motivational Energy unleashes the Power of ME. ME as in the Motivational Energy that is inside of YOU — unique, individual, one of a kind You. The ME within the true You is an incredible source of power. Use it, build on it, unleash it!

When you identify and focus on your Core Strengths, you are giving them Active Attention. When you invest time and effort to understand and cultivate these talents, this power within you, you create natural excitement and energy that comes from doing what you love and loving what you're doing. It is an excitement that feeds on itself, creating passion, adrenalin and positive energy. Have you ever been so involved in doing something that the hours just flew by? Have you ever worked on a project that was more fun than work, because you found the subject, or even the process, intoxicating? Have you ever learned or participated in something for the very first time and found that you had a natural talent or a surprising passion for it?

This happened to me a few summers ago, when I attended a weekend program for women that focused on developing outdoor skills. It was there that I first discovered that I was a 'natural shot' with both a revolver and a semi-automatic pistol. From the very first shot with a .22 caliber 'plinker' to the progressively larger rounds I shot that day, I nailed the targets in tight little groups, time and time again.

I had clearly uncovered a talent and an interest that I didn't know that I possessed until that weekend. And yes, it did become a passion. I came home and took private lessons at the local gun club and attended a three-day shooting camp. These days, I go to the club a few times a month to stay in practice, blow off a few rounds and get rid of a lot of stress. The shooting class I took in Prescott during that women's weekend opened the door to a new lifelong interest and passion for me. I found something that I was good at and I loved the confidence that it gave me. I liked being good at something — who doesn't? — which motivated me to want to get even better. Focusing on the positive feelings made them even stronger. It fueled my new passion.

Discovering something that we are good at is a confidence builder. We feel capable and competent and we like the feeling, so we actively look for ways to spend more time using and building on our new skill. We like the idea of being 'really good at something'. It makes us feel talented and able, and when we feel talented and able, we feel strong. Strength creates confidence, and confidence can be very, very contagious. When we believe in ourselves, others will do the same. If we don't, they won't. Remember, they can only see what we put out to the world. If we project positive energy, they see and feel positive energy. If we speak and act negatively or mope around, that's exactly what they'll see.

Motivational Energy Explained

Motivational Energy is the positive, highly magnetic energy that we project when we focus on and amplify our true Core Strengths. Creating this energy is a multi-step process. The simplicity of the process is fairly impressive, given the power of the energy that is created. It's similar to how electricity makes a light bulb burn brightly, another amazingly simple process that generates bright, beneficial energy.

Think about how a light bulb works. It creates and projects light by converting electrical energy to light energy. Now think about how power gets to that light bulb in the first place. Energy (electrons) travels through a conduit along a one-way path from a source (a circuit) to a site where the energy leaves the circuit (a return) and produces an action, or reaction, through a connection. The part of an electrical circuit that is between the electron's starting point and the point at which they return to the source is called the load.

A traditional light bulb is actually composed of very few parts. These include two metal contacts which connect to the ends of an electrical circuit. These are typically a foot contact and an insulated screw thread contact (that screws into the receptacle of, let's say, a lamp). The contacts are connected to two stiff wires which are, in turn, attached to a thin metal filament, usually made of tungsten. The filament is positioned in the center of the bulb and held in place by a mounting made of glass. The glass covering that houses the structure gives it its bulb-like shape. The oxygen in the structure is removed and replaced with a chemically inert gas such as argon, which slows down the evaporation of the filament. (Tungsten is flammable and would burn up if there was oxygen available. Thomas Edison perfected a process for extracting all of the oxygen from the bulb. That was *the real secret* to inventing the light bulb.) The presence of the argon prevents heated tungsten atoms from bounding away from the filament, thus prolonging the life of the bulb. Longer-lasting bulbs use a better quality of gas, often krypton, which is also more expensive. Six components and a shot of gas represent the sum total of a light bulb's parts, regardless of its wattage. Pretty impressive for the outcome, don't you think?

Okay, now here comes the science. When the bulb is in place and the lamp is hooked up to a power supply, electric current flows from one contact to the other, then through the wires and to the filament. That filament has a lot of resistance built into it, which creates friction — and heat — as the power moves through it. Current is basically the mass movement of free electrons moving from a negatively charged area to a positive one. Along the way, they play 'bumper cars' with the tungsten atoms of the filament, which heat up in reaction. As the atoms heat up, electrical energy is converted to light energy and the filament begins to glow. How brightly depends on the temperature level that is reached. The filaments of most household bulbs (75 or 100 watts) heat up to about 4,600 degrees Fahrenheit (about 2,500 degrees Celsius). No wonder a light bulb feels hot to the touch! Temperatures like these produce a lot of thermal radiation. (Flouresecent bulbs lose far less energy to heat emission and are therefore much more efficient.)

A lot of elements have to be in place before a bulb will light. A source of electricity has to be available and accessible with a complete, unbroken circuit in place to provide a consistent flow of energy. A switch or other means of turning the power on and off has to be in place, as does an outlet to connect to. Fuses and circuit breakers must be in place along the route to keep the system working safely. The bulb should in good working order and ready to shine. And then there will be light!

The principle of Motivational Energy works in much the same way. A source of power must be available, along with a strategy for accessing it. Identifying and focusing on the power source amplifies it and channels it in a positive direction, toward a point where it can be projected outward. Flipping the switch to the 'on' position pushes the energy out toward its target. The greater the level of focus and Active Attention that is applied throughout the pipeline (the conduit), the greater the level of energy that will be created.

The greater the level of energy that is created, the more brightly the bulb will shine — the more brightly YOU will shine.

Motivational Energy (ME) is the power source that exists internally to help us achieve our personal and professional goals. ME draws from our Core Strengths and creates available, accessible energy that can be channeled and targeted. It is the power that is generated by identifying, amplifying and giving Active Attention to our Core Strengths.

The creation of Motivation Energy (ME) takes places in six steps:

1) Identify your Core Strengths;

2) Amplify your Core Strengths by focusing and building on them;

3) Channel the positive Energy that is created in a productive, targeted direction driven by your personal or professional goals. Creating a clear set of goals provides the first section of Conduit, which completes the circuit and leads to the Switch;

4) Project your Motivational Energy outward by 'Flipping the Switch'. The Switch is the directed attention and effort that you apply;

5) Active Attention propels the energy through the second section of the Conduit and toward its intended audience. Movement through this second section of conduit occurs as you implement the strategies and tactics that you have devised to help you reach your goals. It requires thought, effort and, yes, work;

6) Targeted Motivational Energy lights the bulb!

You are the Bulb. When Motivational Energy pulses through you, you light up with purpose and confidence. You become filled with enthusiasm and excitement as you realize your strengths and your true potential. You radiate from the positive energy that is building within you and projecting outward. You begin to attract the types of people and circumstances that you need in your life to achieve your goals because you are focused — and completely confident — in your ability to achieve a positive outcome.

And it shows.

The positive reinforcement of having things 'go your way' creates even more energy and your bulb burns even brighter. You'll literally move faster with a proverbial 'spring in your step' that results from the energy pulsating within you. There's a reason why some people seem to have a natural radiance and glow about them or why some people never seem to see the cup as anything but half full (and rising!). People who are optimistic are confident about themselves and the future. They have an 'I can do it' attitude that appears to come from some source of inner strength, and they know how to project it forward.

Motivational Energy is that source. Everyone is born with it. Everyone can learn to cultivate it. Everyone can learn to *Be the Bulb!* Let's look at a visual explanation of how the process works.

Diagram 1

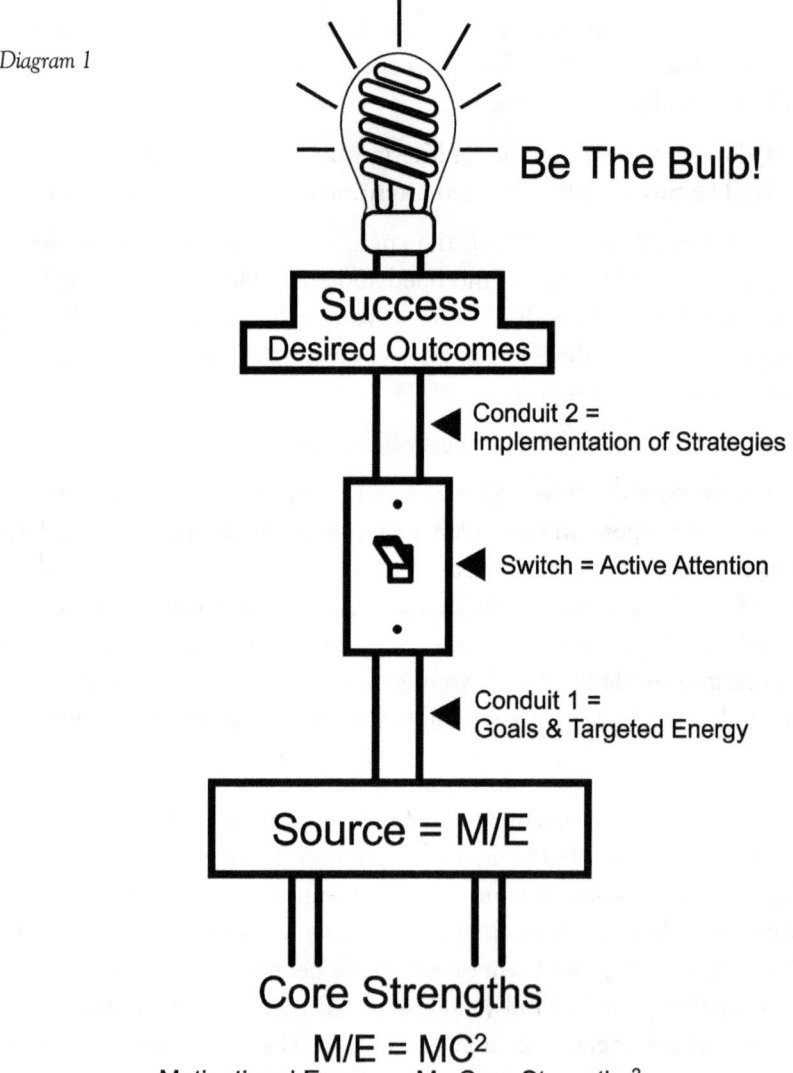

Be The Bulb!

Success
Desired Outcomes

◀ Conduit 2 = Implementation of Strategies

◀ Switch = Active Attention

◀ Conduit 1 = Goals & Targeted Energy

Source = M/E

Core Strengths

$M/E = MC^2$
Motivational Energy = My Core Strengths^2

Identifying (Step 1) and Amplifying (Step 2) your Core Strengths (the Source) creates and propels energy outward as you devise a plan to reach your goals. Even just working on your plan will create positive energy. Having goals is the key to creating motivation. When we're filled with energy and purpose, it's easier to get up in the morning and get started on our day. When we feel like we 'have a plan', we are more confident and eager to get started. And when we know where we're going — and have a plan for getting there — we are more likely to come across (and be receptive to) information, opportunities and resources that can help get us where we want to go.

When we apply Active Attention and actively implement our strategies or 'plan', we can't help but make progress toward our goals. Yes, we may still run into roadblocks along the way, but the momentum that we are building will encourage us to seek out solutions or devise new strategies. Creativity soars when positive energy builds. We become open to ideas that we may not have considered before. Our glass is half full, not half empty, and we fully expect it to fill up. Optimists are fueled by an inner energy source that even the most pessimistic nay-sayers can't put out. Charismatic people attract others in much the same way. They make the most of their natural strengths and talents and are confident in their skin. Others are attracted to their confidence. They want to bask in their energy and light.

There's room for a little more science right here. Einstein's Theory of Relativity, the $e = mc^2$ that the Motivational Energy equation is modeled after, explains how mass is converted to energy. Matter and energy are really just different forms of the same concept. Matter can be turned into energy and vice versa.

Think of your Core Strengths as positive matter that you possess inside yourself. Putting that matter 'out there' by focusing Active Attention on your strengths converts that matter into energy. Likewise, that energy can — and will — come back to you and make your strengths or passions even stronger. How? Through the positive reinforcement you get from a job well done, making progress toward your goals, coming up with an exciting new idea or strategy, or by attracting the types of people and opportunities that you are looking for. All of these create positive energy and confidence and you move forward with even stronger steps. Positive energy attracts positive energy. In that way, the Motivational Energy that you create becomes self-feeding and fulfilling. Once you get it going, it attracts its own fuel source — no energy company or power utility needed!

Here's another one: Sir Isaac Newton's First Law of Motion states that 'Every body perseveres in its state of being at rest or of moving uniformly straight ahead, except insofar as it is compelled to change its state by forces impressed.' (Source: Cohen and Whitman 1999 translation of Newton's concept.) In other words, when you push toward and against something, it pushes back. For every action there is a reaction. If you push positive energy outward, the positive energy it finds will push back toward you.

It all begins at the Source, the creation of the initial positive energy. Your first learning opportunity comes when you look inside yourself to Identify your Core Strengths. The second opportunity comes when you devise a strategy to capitalize and build on them. This is when you are preparing to 'put it out there', by learning, by focusing, and by laying out your plans. It is a slower, building stage, but a very important one. When we talk about doing 'foundation work' (whether in life or construction), we are referring to the basic research and groundwork that must be done in order to get any project off to the best possible start. It is very necessary, but it is not enough on its own to lead to the realization of your goals or directly to success.

You will learn how to look inside yourself and Identify your Core Strengths shortly. It is not a difficult or impossible process by any means, but it really is just the first step. If you have bought this book and have been reading so far thinking that I am going to hand you a one-step-and-you're-done solution, you are bound to be disappointed. Unlike the infomercials that promise you easy wealth with little work or the books that tell you that wishing and willing good things to happen will make your dreams come true, the concept of Motivational Energy requires effort and work on your part. You can not *Be the Bulb!* unless you 1) know what you want from life; 2) know what you're good at and what you have to work with; 3) are willing to focus on your strengths and passions, instead of just your daily 'to do' list; and 4) have developed a plan to get you where you want to go. Does it require effort? Yes. Is it worth it? Yes. It is important, inner-directed, very productive work that will serve you well no matter what you choose to do throughout your life. Knowing yourself, your needs and your strengths is always a good investment. Otherwise, finding happiness, fulfillment and yes, success, become accidental occurrences at best. Knowing what you want and need enables you to successfully seek these things out and *create them*. At the very least, it helps you keep your eyes open to potentially life-changing or fulfilling opportunities that cross your path. If you don't know what you're looking for, how can you possibly know when you've found it? If you don't know what makes you feel happy and fulfilled, how can you begin to look for people, projects, careers or even relationships that will make you feel happy, successful and fulfilled? If you don't know what you want to do with your life, how will you know when you have finally found your life's work?

By focusing on your Core Strengths, Motivational Energy helps you realize what you want and need from life so that you can devise a plan to go after it. That's work worth doing, in anyone's book.

When you're doing something that you truly love and when you can feel your goals and dreams moving closer with every step that you take, it feels nothing like work. After nearly 30 years of doing things that I liked, but maybe didn't always love, I am finally focusing on my true interests and strengths every day. And for the first time, purpose and passion have come together and I feel like I am truly living my life instead of just working my way through it on a daily basis. Motivational Energy kept my bulb lit and propelled me through the first half of my career by seeking out challenges and opportunities that fed my inner needs. I am one of those people who is naturally fueled by my inner passions. I was creating and projecting Motivational Energy for decades before I realized what was happening. Once I became aware of what really 'rang my chimes' and made my energy and enthusiasm soar, I began to actively seek out clients, activities and projects that fed those interests. My energy level soared even higher and I realized that my excitement, my enthusiasm and my confidence were attracting even more of what I wanted in my life. I was attracting the types of clients I wanted to work with and was being sought out for the kinds of projects that I liked best. I was confident, optimistic and excited about the future and guess what? The world around me was excited as well. Enthusiasm and positive energy truly are contagious.

Being aware of the power and the potential that you have within yourself is the critical first step and it is a very empowering one. You have to take a good look at yourself and who you really are, not just your public persona, but as a true individual with your own set of strengths and talents and quirks and idiosyncrasies that may or may not be seeing light on a daily basis.

Identifying and creating a plan to Amplify those strengths requires more thought, some perseverance and a little creativity. This is where you begin lining up your resources and creating a foundation to build on. This is where you start creating the 'infrastructure' of your plan for success. This is where you'll climb inside and outside the box and think all the way around it. This is where your entrepreneurial instincts — and some marketing creativity — will kick in. Amplification is where you will put your energy into words and begin to build on it. You will lay a framework to channel that energy, through conduit that directs it toward your goals and intentions, and prepare yourself to actively achieve the success you are looking for.

Nothing will happen, however, until you actually Flip the Switch, until you take action and apply Active Attention. Flipping the Switch is where you begin to actively put yourself out there. It is where, for the first time, you are showing the world what you intend to do, *by doing it!*

Flipping the Switch requires courage and a true desire to succeed at doing something that you really want to do or by achieving a highly desired goal. Motivation is the element that pushes the switch upward.

Imagine what it must be like to step out of an airplane when you sky dive for the first time. You know that once you step out, there is no turning back. You are committed to finishing what you have begun. I often put myself in situations like this (though I have yet to jump out of my first airplane!). Sometimes I really want to do or try something and I know that it is a good step for me, but some element of fear or uncertainty is causing me to 'waffle' or procrastinate. I overcome this by moving myself forward one step at a time, until I am virtually at the point of no return. (In the business world, this means getting to the point where rescheduling, cancelling or just not showing up would be disastrous.) My career involves giving talks and presentations to groups of various sizes. When I'm in a familiar group, no problem. When it's a new audience at a venue where I am not familiar with the setting, the equipment or the 'atmosphere', my comfort level isn't quite as high. I will over-prepare (which is a good idea anyway) and stress myself out over whether I will be able to work the equipment seamlessly and talk effortlessly without clinging to my back up notes. (Even though I know from experience that neither one is ever a problem in the end.) At the same time I also know that, if I take one step at a time and continually move myself closer to the time of whatever I have to do or whomever I have to see, at some point I will actually be walking into the room — or the appointment, the meeting, the sales call, whatever — and my 'fight or flight' response will take over. I brought (okay, sometimes pushed) myself to the point of no return and placed myself in a situation where I must perform. My adrenalin soars as I prepare to 'survive' the situation and I go into my high-energy, master presenter mode.

This strategy has been so consistently successful that I know, with confidence, what the end result will be. This is actually the type of high-pressure situation in which I do my best work and it is that confidence that carries me through, every time.

Flipping the Switch requires courage but it is also a great confidence builder. You have to push past any fears or qualms that you may have and choose to begin. Preparing to act is one thing. Many people are very good at that and spend much of their lives 'preparing to succeed'. Taking action is quite another. When you are ready to take action, you are ready to succeed. You are ready to move forward. You are confident and strong enough to do what you have to do to reach your goals. You are ready.

Flipping the Switch is the tough part, but it will be the turning point in your strategy. It creates the momentum you need to move forward. If you have ever had to make a difficult decision in your life, if you have ever had to say something or do something that required some amount of courage, if you have ever been willing to take a risk in order to take a chance on getting something that you really wanted, then you can do this. Flipping the Switch is the challenge. Once you do it, once you take action, momentum builds as your energy swells. That confidence that we've been talking about? It soars. You will feel capable, confident and committed to going further. You have stepped off the airplane, with confidence, and you have never felt so exhilarated in your life.

Here's another confidence builder: there's really very little risk involved in Flipping the Switch. Only you really know the level of work and preparation that has gone into preparing you for the moment when you begin to actively 'put yourself out there'. Only you really know what the end result is supposed to be. Others will notice that something is different. They will see what is, at first, a subtle but positive difference in you and your work. They will begin to look at you in a different, more interested way. They may even begin to pay attention to you for the very first time.

But they won't quite be able to put their fingers on why that is, unless you tell them. They won't know that you are actively putting a true and stronger 'real' you forward, unless you make a point of announcing your plans. They will notice that you appear happier, more energized and interesting and they will feel themselves drawn to you, but they won't know why that is. They may ask you if something has changed or why you suddenly seem so excited and happy. There is no need to explain. Just smile and say 'Life is good', *because it is* — and it's about to get even better.

So there really is very little risk involved in Flipping the Switch. Only you know what is supposed to be happening. Only you will be the judge of whether you are satisfied with the results. Only you will make the decision on how fast or how slow to go. Flipping the Switch typically will, however, encourage you to move forward faster as your energy builds, your confidence increases and you crave more of the progress that you can already feel.

Let's go back to the Motivational Energy diagram for a moment. The speed of your progress, the rate at which your positive energy builds, will increase as your energy is directed through this next phase and toward its targets. This, quite literally, is where the pace picks up. Once you put positive energy out there, it begins to build on itself. Things naturally move forward faster.

Motivational Energy Explained

During the first phase of your work, inside the first section of Conduit, if you will, things progress at your own pace. They can move quickly or slowly. You haven't put anything out into the marketplace yet. You can proceed at whatever rate works best for you. You don't have to Flip the Switch until you are good and ready. You don't have to step out of the airplane until you have made sure that your chute is in good working order. You don't have to debut the Brand until you are sure that the Brand is ready for prime time.

Once you put your energy out into the world, you will still have the ability to control it. You can pull your energy back or you can tune it down. You can moderate the speed at which you are moving forward. You can, and should, control where your energy is directed and who and what it attracts. Targeting is very important to reaching your goals. So is gatekeeping, and we will discuss both of these critical issues shortly. For now, just keep in mind this rule that marketing and advertising professionals live by: Your resources, or energy, will go further and be more efficient and effective if you focus your efforts specifically on a designated audience and goal. Broadcasting your positive energy and light to the greater marketplace without distinction will increase the *quantity* of what life brings to you (because you are generally more Visible), but it may not move you closer to your specific goals. You may not be Found by those whom you need and want to attract the most.

Focusing your energy on strategies and tactics that are specifically designed to help you reach your goals will move you forward faster. Concentrating on what you want and need and building energy to specifically achieve those goals will attract the people and events and opportunities that will help you move forward and can get you where you want to go in a much shorter timeframe. Devising strategies to help you achieve this is where the marketing element comes in. Remember our discussion of strength-based branding? Strong brands have detailed brand strategies that guide their success. Creating such a strategy creates the conduit that will direct your efforts. It leads you toward the point where you are well-armed and ready to take action. Direct your energy at your target and be selective on what you let come back to you. Targeting channels your energy in the most productive direction. Gatekeeping is another important strategy that I will talk about at length in Chapter 9. Effective gatekeeping filters out unproductive or negative energy that can actually keep you from reaching your goals. It helps keeps your light strong by steering you away from negative people and situations that can drain your energy or cause you to project it in an unproductive direction. It is a very important subject.

Harnessing Motivational Energy really is comparable to the simplicity of a light bulb. Plug into your energy source, channel the power, actively project it and build on it and your Bulb will burn brightly. Now it's time to start building your energy source.

Part II: How to Be the Bulb, Step by Step

Chapter 4
Creating the Source

Each of us is unique. We each possess unique strengths, capabilities, talents and interests that, when taken together, create a true representation of who we are. These Core Strengths are within us, they exist, whether we choose to acknowledge them or build on them or not. They may or may not be related to what you are doing now, either in your work or your leisure time, but they are there. Often they are laying dormant and unused. It is time to discover those strengths and welcome them into your current life. It is time to put them to work to build a business, pursue a new interest or a lifelong dream and improve the quality of your life. It is time to turn on the light and get to work.

Motivational Energy occurs when you identify, amplify and channel those strengths in a positive direction. Inner light is created which expands and overflows to your outer personality. The deeper you delve and work, the more effort you will produce. The truer your focus and your goals, the brighter your light will shine. Focus is what gets you what you want. Applying effort creates the energy you need to make it happen. Channeling that energy and targeting it at what you want will bring that goal within reach by attracting 'suddenly apparent' opportunities, new or newly interesting people and the occurrence of seemingly chance or random events that are relevant to what you are looking for. Call it synchronicity or luck or what you will, but the bottom line is this: You will find that which you actively seek and are open to. You will not realize true success unless you are ready (and willing) to recognize opportunities to be successful when they cross your path.

You will attract what you want in your life, NOT because you have uncovered some secret and the universe is suddenly working in your favor but because you are now better prepared — and ready — to recognize and attract what you want and need. When you are focused and have a plan, when you are working that plan and seeing results, when your confidence is building and you are excited about what you are doing, you cannot help but succeed. When your Bulb is shining brightly, you are emitting positive energy that lights up the area around you. The world looks brighter because *you* are brighter. You know what you want and what you are looking for and your (growing) energy is helping you find it. Your positive energy is shining light on new opportunities and options. You can't help but see things clearer. *They are clearer.*

A Core Strength is a natural interest or talent. It's something that you are inherantly good at or a topic that you find yourself drawn to, time and time again. It is an activity that you make time for and look forward to. It is a skill that you find effortless, and require very little direction to learn. It is a task that feels more like a hobby than work.

A Core Strength is one of the unique pieces that are part of each of us. And although we may share interests (football!) and talents (shooting!) with others, we each bring our own individual spin or style to its pursuit. We are attracted to people who share our strengths, have similar interests or participate in similar types of work. Like seeks like because we prefer to place ourselves in situations where we can indulge our interests and practice our strengths, among people who share our passions. When we build a business this way, it will also be fulfilling — and successful.

There are dozens, probably hundreds of books that can take you through an assessment process to determine what you have an affinity for, what you are good at and what type of entrepreneurial personality fits you best. My advice? Read a couple of them (any bookstore is packed with them) and then put them aside. Or do some intensive research online, read a variety of articles and take the online versions of those same assessment tests. Use what you learn about introspection, need assessment and personality, maybe do an exercise or two, then spend some time to *just think*. Think about what gets you excited and interested. Think about what causes you to jump out of bed in the morning in a hurry to start your day. Think about what you used to love to do when you were younger, whenever you have free time, when no one else is paying attention or whenever the responsibilities of the 'real world' are not knocking at your door. When the choice is yours to make, what do you choose to do with your (very) precious time? If money were no object, what would you choose to do each day? Think, and focus, on these activities and interests. This is where it all begins.

These are your passions. These are your Core Strengths.

Core Strengths are pesky little things that pop up time and time again, whether we pay attention to them or not. Many of your 'brilliant' ideas will be related to an interest that you have. You will do some of your best work when you are immersed in a project that utilizes or is even remotely related to a Core Strength skill. Each of us has Core Strengths, whether we realize it, or cultivate them, or not. In an earlier chapter, you heard me use a similar phrase in regard to personal brands: Each of us has a personal brand, whether we realize it, or work at it, or not. It's true in both cases. Just because we do not recognize something or actively pay attention to it does not mean that it does not exist. We live in a world where many people are going about their day-to-day business without recognizing the exceptional talents or strengths that they have; without making the most of those talents; and without putting their best skills to work. So many of us are taught the same set of life and social skills and learn from the same general book of knowledge. We are taught how to take care of ourselves by making a living, but we are not taught how to make a life. There are (too) few opportunities to develop 'non-essential' skills or interests for many of us and, when they do occur, we tend to think of these skills or interests as 'hobbies'. If we recognize our Core Strengths, we rarely give them the attention and respect that they deserve. We are too busy taking care of business or life matters to give them their due.

There is an entire industry that is based on helping you discover your Core Strengths and competencies. Whether or not you feel you need to seek out the services of a life coach or other developmental consultant is up to you. Many of us already have a pretty fair idea of what we're good it. We know what gets us excited (or used to get us excited when we paid attention to it) and can come up with at least a general description of how we'd prefer to spend our days, if we had the chance. We gravitate to situations and people who provide a 'taste' of that experience, a taste that can tide us over until we actually get there. Focus on those strengths and interests now, as you work through the process. You can dig deeper and choose more carefully later, if you feel that you are on the wrong track for some reason.

It is important to focus on building on your Core Strengths and not on trying to overcome or 'fix' your weaknesses; to focus on your positives, instead of your negatives. Positive, magnetic energy is created by focusing on and fueling positive, high-potential strengths. Be a builder, not a remodeler. See what can be, instead of what needs to be fixed. You will achieve the greatest success and the greatest satisfaction by putting energy into, and taking energy from, that which you are passionate about.

No one is passionate about their weaknesses. And if they are, that's another story — and another book.

Confidence comes from focusing on strengths and capabilities (or core competencies, as they say like to say in business schools). And remember, confidence is an entrepreneur's most powerful tool. Confidence is what makes success seem possible, in business and in life. Focus on that which gives you confidence. Arm yourself with the best chance possible. Don't make this harder than it has to be.

Here are some additional guidelines for assessing your strengths:

What are you good at? What skills do you utilize on a daily basis, in your job or otherwise? Which do you find easiest or most satisfying to use? What puts a smile on your face and makes you feel good? What makes the hours fly by without notice? What talents or skills do people most often compliment you on?

Which of your achievements are you proudest of and what skills or strengths did you have to draw from to make them happen? Your experiences, both in life and business, are a source of information that you cannot afford to ignore. Use them as a starting point and take a trip far down memory lane. Your Core Strengths may have been clearest (and some would say purest) when you were much younger, long before adult responsibilities (or input) took over.

Be specific in considering and inventorying your Core Strengths. You are not looking for general qualities or personality traits such as optimistic, resilient, brave or kind – although these are all admirable qualities to have.

Create a list of specific, actionable interests, skills and strengths that you could conceivably build a business on. Qualities are very important to building your Motivational Energy, but they are not the Source of that energy. This is an important distinction that you should keep in mind throughout the process: Source = Strengths, Qualities = Message/Delivery. We will learn more about message delivery in a later chapter.

Also try to distinguish between true passion and a passing fancy. Core Strengths are built on true interests and passions that are inherent to who you are. Life-changing decisions should not be made on whims or fads or lukewarm interest. Look for something that truly trips your trigger, not just something that is socially acceptable, trendy or popular.

Take your time at this stage. Everything that you do from this point forward will be based on the work you do during this identifying stage. Passion, excitement and purpose comes from digging deep, doing the work and determining where your truest strengths and interests lie. Remember that: Dig deep, do the work, determine your strengths. You will know when you have uncovered the core. You will feel it when you are on the right path. Core Strengths create energy and excitement creates energy. You will know when you have hit the mark because the energy, and the ideas, will begin to flow.

Something else to remember: Your goal is to create a business and a life that is richly focused on your Core Strengths, but not exclusively by any means. I am a huge believer in lifelong learning and, in order to grow, you have to be willing to step outside of your comfort zone regularly and explore what lies beyond it. You have to be able to face your fears and venture into the unknown, to try things you have never done before and to be open to new experiences. Focusing on your Core Strengths creates Motivational Energy, but those strengths alone won't be enough to keep your Bulb burning brightly. Learning, growth, creativity — and evolution — will all be essential to your continued ability to attract what (and who) you want and need for your business and yourself (and we will talk more about all of these in later chapters). Yes, you should invest your energy and your effort in what has the potential to provide the greatest level of results and satisfaction, but never assume that the person who you are today is the only person you are ever going to be. That would be far too limiting. Your goals and your priorities may change — as may your definition of success and satisfaction — even though your inherent Core Strengths will not. Be open to evolution and change. Be open to taking your strengths to the next level. And: Don't assume that you have inventoried every one of your Core Strengths (or that you have to). Be open to new opportunities, not just for success, but for learning and discovery. It would be very presumptuous to think that you or I or anyone could create an inventory of our innermost, truest strengths in one sitting, or even one period of time. Exploration (and introspection) should be an ongoing and an evolutionary process. Always think of yourself, and your life, *as a work in progress.*

This book is your opportunity. This moment is the starting point, where you finally take the time to identify, recognize and cultivate the Core Strengths that are not only the driving force behind who you are, but also have the potential to be the foundation for a truly well-rounded, fulfilling life-work existence. Focusing on those strengths will create the Motivational Energy — ME — that you need to move towards your goals. Putting that energy out there and actively applying it toward what you want to do and who you want to be will put the power of ME to work to light up your life by creating energy, interest and confidence — and not just in yourself, but in others who come in contact with your light. *Being the Bulb! means harnessing the Power of ME.*

Motivational Energy equals the Power of ME: my strengths, my passion, my purpose. If you think of Motivational Energy as Passion with a Purpose, you will be off to a very strong start indeed.

I coach CEOs, corporate executives and companies on their images and brands. It is a big part of what I do. Focus and Passion are essential to business success, regardless of whether you are a new small business or a large corporation. Passion is the embodiment of Desire and Intention. It is the fuel that fires us up and makes us want to succeed. Passion is also at the core of Enthusiasm, which is magnetic in its ability to draw others toward us. Always be the Positive One, even when you're delivering unhappy news. Be the guardian of the 'silver lining'. There always is a silver lining. Be the visionary, the positive visionary, who can see what that lining is and continue to create forward momentum based on that potential.

Despite the talk of desires and intentions, creating and projecting Motivational Energy has little to do with attraction theories, at least in their currently popular 'wish and wait' form. Motivational Energy is based on marketing, effective communication, branding and target marketing strategies that have been used by advertisers for years. If you've read Dale Carnegie or Napoleon Hill, you know that each of us can be our own best friend as well as our own worst enemy. We hold the power to help ourselves, or hurt ourselves, more than any other person that we know. Our actions have the greatest potential to influence our success. If we act in a positive, productive manner, we will make progress toward our goals. If we apply energy and effort to our actions, they will move us forward more quickly. If we target our efforts at a specific goal, instead of diffusing our effort by broadcasting it to the world in general, we are more likely to achieve what we want and we are more likely to actually reach, and grasp, our goal. There is nothing secretive or mystical about any of this.

The first step is to focus on ME and to build on it. So, how do you get started?

The entire premise of this book is based on attracting the people and opportunities that you need to be successful in your chosen calling. Be open to those opportunities. They may not be exactly what you expect. Focus and build on your strengths, but leave room for exploration, for adventure and for growth. True confidence comes from tackling the unknown, and 'living to tell the story'. Step outside your comfort zone and strive to create new boundaries and explore new limits. The light created by your Motivational Energy, your Bulb, will guide you and give you the confidence that you need to proceed.

And remember: Success is not accidental. You have to make it happen and you have to look for opportunities to make it happen. The same policy applies to identifying and building on your Core Strengths. No one is going to do the work if you don't. The answer is not going to suddenly 'come' to you. Waiting for a sign or a moment of clarity is not going to make it happen. You have to create your own clarity. You have to create your own moment. Usually, our 'revelations' are revealing what we already know. They are unveiling what is already in our subconscious, or our past, or our heart. Defining your Core Strengths takes Desire and Action (does that sound familiar?), *not wishing or wanting or waiting.* Your moment is now, but only if you choose to make now. Only if you choose to make it happen.

Choose to begin looking for opportunities to succeed and grow. *Choose to begin now.*

Each of us has the power to make choices, choices that will make our lives better or worse. Regardless of what your life is like right now, good or bad, you have the power to make choices that can make it better. The power to choose what is right for you belongs to you and only to you, and that is exactly the way that it should be. Only you truly know what you want and need from life. Only you can choose if, how and when to go after it. Only you can decide where you want to be, how you're going to get there, and who you're going to take with you on the most important journey of your life. You are the only person who has the power to make these choices. You are the only person who can choose to be comfortable with the choices that you make. You are the only person who can determine what your real needs and goals are, whether you will pursue them and whether you will stay true to them throughout your life. Each of us creates our own reality through the choices that we make on a daily basis. Whether or not it is the reality that we truly want, we have a hand in it, just the same. Choose carefully but, most importantly, *choose to begin.*

What we accomplish in life has everything to do with who we truly are, beneath the trappings of life and its circumstances and all of the must's and must not's that we have been taught or modeled since we were very young. Self-discovery is the starting point. Self-acceptance is the destination. Until we can really see ourselves for who we are, we will be blinded to the possibilities of who we can be, and what we can create — in business and in life. Identifying and amplifying your Core Strengths is the all-important beginning.

Chapter 5
Turning On the Light

Identifying your Core Strengths is not enough. You must also work to Amplify them. Amplification occurs when your focus on a Core Strength and devote time and attention to nurturing its growth. You have acknowledged it as a calling or a passion and are putting it front and center, where it belongs. You are preparing to build on it and to broadcast it to the world. Focusing on and Amplifying your Core Strengths is the second step in the process of creating Motivational Energy.

When you focus on your Core Strengths, you are putting your best foot forward. You are creating positive energy that will attract more of the same. You are inviting opportunities that will relate to your passion. You will begin attracting people who can become your benefactors, your mentors, your partners or your customers. You are creating a reality that is strength-based, focused and proactive. You are creating momentum. You are creating a life.

As entrepreneurs, we long to turn those passions into income-generating businesses. Who doesn't dream of being able to wake up each day and make money for living their passion? A business that is built on your strengths is much more likely to succeed and it is much more likely to survive the challenges that all new businesses face. Why? Because its entrepreneurial, passion-pursuing owner, you, will be more likely to hang in there, work hard and do what it takes to make it through tough times. Your commitment and emotional investment will make you willing to invest your time and effort to make things work and the quality of the time and the effort that you invest will be better. You will be involved by choice, and choice is the most powerful motivator in the world.

Remember: If you believe in yourself the world will agree. The same can be said for your business. When you are passionate about your work, your passion will be contagious. When you are confident about your products and services, potential customers will be attracted to that confidence. They will be more apt to listen, and to hear, what you are saying. Think back to our discussion of strong brands. Strong brands are clear and presented consistently. They are founded on benefits, not attributes and they are promoted through messaging which speaks to prospects in a voice and tone that they can relate to. Amplifying your Core Strengths works exactly the same way.

A personal branding strategy puts your energy into words and provides a framework to amplify your strengths. You do not have to be a writer to create one. Your personal branding strategy should complete this phrase: 'When people think of me or hear my name, I want them to think of ......'. The answer is the foundation of your branding strategy, which will be very similar in theory to the branding strategies that are created for products.

Having a personal branding strategy will also enable you to make choices that are *consistent with your goals*. It will keep you focused and on track and will make it easier to be a Good Gatekeeper. Think of it as the conduit that channels your energy in the most productive direction: toward your desired goals.

The brand development process derives benefits (positive energy) from attributes (Core Strengths) and creates a meaningful, marketable strategy that promises to fulfill a need or solve a problem for your target customers. Remember, strong brands are distinctive, relevant and consistent. Distinctive brands differentiate themselves in some way. They set their products, companies or people apart from the competition and above the crowd. Relevant brands resonate with the target audience by zeroing in on an important need or desire. If your brand fulfills a relevant promise, others will be drawn to it and you. Consistent brands deliver as expected and grow stronger with time. And: You only get credit for what you do consistently. Repeated interaction which is supported by consistent delivery that is in keeping with the brand's promise will reinforce your brand. Positive word of mouth will grow. Viral marketing will commence. Your reputation will precede you as people come to 'know' of you and the value that you deliver. (Value has little to do with price and much more to do with *satisfaction*. It is about providing what people need, want and expect at a price that they are willing to pay.) Your brand will fuel your efforts forward, while attracting customers and opportunities your way.

A personal branding strategy puts your Core Strengths into words and makes it easier to Amplify them. Use these guidelines to incorporate the strong, new foundation you are creating into every part of your personal and professional life:

- Think about all of the ways that one or all of your Core Strengths can be put to use, in business and in life. For example, if you are incredibly organized, think about the many ways in which being organized can become a viable, successful business. The project management and event planning industries are populated by successful entrepreneurs who are organized and obsessed with detail. That obsession however, is not enough. There also has to be a need in the marketplace, and a passion to want to fulfill that need and succeed. Identify the best use of your Core Strengths and create a list of potential and, hopefully, pressing customer needs that utilize one or a combination of your true strengths.

- Make an active, committed decision to focus on the strength (or strengths) that you have decided to build and pursue. Accept it, embrace it and make it part of your identity. Put it front and center, where it belongs. It will evolve as you do.

- Amplification requires consistent, ongoing attention and promotion. Make your Core Strength the focus of your day and life. Incorporate it into everything that you do. Look for information and opportunities that relate to it. Make it your priority. Make it part of your identity. This is supposed to be all about you. Make sure that it is, on a daily basis.

- Demonstrate commitment to your strength by actively investing time and resources to nurturing it. Begin to accumulate the information, knowledge, training and resources you need to create a successful business. Commit your own resources. If you have limited financial resources, invest your time in finding what you need. You have to be willing to invest in yourself in some way before others will be willing to do the same. Confidence is key.

- Create a message that puts your passion into words, if only to inspire yourself at this point. Write it down and post it where you can see it daily. Share it with others as a fait accompli (done deal). Don't say 'I'm thinking about' or 'I may' or even 'I could'. Use powerful action phrases such as 'I am', 'I will' and 'I want'. Think and speak confidently and you will be confident.

- Don't say it loudly, say it strongly and with passion and purpose. Making noise is not enough. There is already plenty of noise in the world. Keep your message clear, strong and meaningful, and put confidence into its delivery. It is the best way to break through the clutter.

- Make your message the massage, which is a play on a phrase popularized by media expert Marshall McLuhan in his 1967 best-selling cult marketing classic, *The Medium is the Massage*, Marshall McLuhan put forth his theory that the way we think and interpret the world will be shaped by the dominant media at the time. According to McLuhan, the technology used to communicate and deliver a message — whether it is print, radio, television, clothing or even graffiti (keep the era in mind) — is as much a part of that message as the words or pictures that are used. In other words, environment plays a huge role in perception. The environment that we place ourselves and our message in adds another level of connotation to our communication. (Think of the social networking sites that you belong to and you'll have a perfect modern day example.) McLuhan's basic premise is still relevant today: Put yourself — and your message — in an appropriate environment, always.

- Be the Brand by focusing on the truest part of yourself: your Core Strengths. This isn't just your livelihood that we're talking about, it's your life. Make sure that your goals for each are well-matched and well-suited to each other from the beginning. It is easier to build life-work balance in from the 'get-go', than it is to create it later.

Goal setting and targeting will ensure that you utilize your energy in the most efficient way possible. The next step in your preparation to Flip the Switch and put your energy into the marketplace is to create a framework that moves you — and your energy — forward in a direct path toward the fulfillment of your goals.

Constructing the Conduit by Setting Goals and Intentions

Think back to our discussion of how energy travels from a source to the light bulb. In order to create light, conduit must lead energy from the source to the point distribution, usually an outlet of some sort. The conduit directs the energy in the desired and appropriate direction so that it can ultimately reach its destination: the bulb.

Motivational Energy works in the same way. Identifying the Source, our Core Strengths, and Amplifying them is not enough. We must also direct the energy that we create toward our goals. In order to be able to do this, *we must know what we want to achieve*. Setting goals and intentions is critical to the success of any effort, whether we are creating a business or a relationship. We must have a strategy for success. Creating that strategy begins with setting goals and intentions that put us on the road to where we want to be. Our goal is to get there — usually in as directly a manner as possible. Conduit, by its nature, is very straight and direct. If you've ever seen the infrastructure of a house before the drywall goes on, you know that the electrical conduit (and the plumbing piping as well) is designed to bring power (or water) to all parts of the house in the most efficient way possible. The lines are straight and direct. They do not meander, or take their time getting to where they need to go.

You will be most successful if you set clear goals and intentions that similarly aim at your target. Your Motivational Energy will be stronger if it is targeted directly at your goals. You will attract what you want faster if you focus on the end result and utilize a strategy that leads you directly to where you want to go in the most efficient way possible. Conduit is that focus and goal setting creates the conduit. Think of it as the 'road' that leads directly to the point where you will send your energy out into the marketplace. Setting clear goals and intentions is equivalent to laying the first segment of conduit.

There are plenty of good books that you can read on goal setting. What follows is a short course in what you need to know to get started, so that you can begin to Amplify your Core Strengths and begin putting the Motivational Energy which that effort creates to work.

Ask yourself these questions: How will I know when I am successful? What will success look like? What will it feel like? How will it fit holistically with all parts of my life? (Business and life success are *not* necessarily the same thing and they can be opposing concepts if you do not make thoughtful choices.) How will I know when I 'have arrived'? And: 'Who will be there to applaud me when I do?'

Each of us has our own unique definition of success. Mine has a lot to do with feeling happy, fulfilled and productive. I am very focused on leaving some type of 'lasting legacy' behind. To me, success treats money as more of a necessity than as a goal of its own. I am not looking to create vast wealth, but it is always nice to be able to pay the bills each month without thinking too much about the process. Your definition of success may be much more focused on wealth and all of the goodies that can come with it. Or it may be focused on ways of providing for yourself or your family that go far beyond putting money in the bank. What matters is that you KNOW what you want in and from life — and not just from one part of your life, but from all of its inter-related areas. Know what your ideal day looks like and feels like. Know how you would spend it, and with whom. Know what you are going after and why and how long you are willing to wait. *You must know what your intentions are in order to achieve them.* You must have a clear understanding, and be able to visualize, what success means and looks like to you. Here's why:

1) The image of your ideal day and of the time when you are living your best life will motivate you to continue working toward your goals. It becomes a goal in itself, and it is a very potent one.

2) You will become more aware of opportunities that can provide you with the resources you need to achieve your goals or lead you faster along the path to success. These opportunities could include learning, financial and relationship resources. They certainly include people whom you meet and places and events that you visit or attend. Opportunity exists everywhere. It is simply a matter of whether or not you are looking for it. You have to be open to opportunity, actively looking for it and willing to

welcome it (and act on it) when it crosses your path. You will be amazed at what you see and find once you begin to actively pay attention.

3) You will become more aware of people who come into your life, either directly or indirectly, who may be able to help you create success. Life is filled with opportunities: people we stand or sit next to, chance meetings, unplanned events, items seen or read, offered projects, ideas that seemingly come out of nowhere. You have to recognize each of them for what they can be if you want to achieve your goals. Consider all of the people whom you meet more carefully and look beyond the face value of the situation in which they appear. Do not pigeonhole anyone too quickly. People who appear to be customers may be mentors. People who appear to be vendors may be partners. Assumptions put roadblocks in the way of opportunity.

Seek out opportunity and work to leverage it into something more. Watch for it. Evaluate it. Answer the door and build on it. Don't let it pass you by. Successful people are constantly watching for opportunity and, when they find it, they embrace it. Why? Because they know that success is not accidental. You have to make it happen and you have to *actively look for opportunities* to make it happen. Don't wait for success to happen. *Make it happen* — one opportunity at a time.

We often hear about being 'on the road to success'. There is no one road to success, but there are a lot of paths and side roads. Knowing which path to take is where strategy comes in. Knowing when to step off the main road and explore a new path is where courage and creativity come in. Knowing when to stop exploring and put the accelerator down in order to get closer to your ultimate destination is where experience comes in. Sometimes you want to explore. Sometimes you just want to get there. In business, we usually want to get there.

Opportunity is a path. It is a road that can move you forward, or present a new direction for achieving your goals. Be aware of and open to possibilities and *then act on them*, as appropriate. **In order to truly be open for business, we have to truly be open to opportunity.**

Keeping your goals top of mind will keep you focused on your goal and will keep you motivated toward achieving your goals. Momentum — forward motion — will be the result.

Committing pen to paper (or fingers to keyboard) is essential. Writing down goals makes them concrete and real and creates a stronger level of commitment. Using images can also be very powerful. I am the proud owner of a full set of Sharpies and an oversized artist's drawing pad, tools that I use to draw charts and colorful lists that help me think through (that's the key part, the thinking through) and define my goals for all parts of my life. The color helps me move beyond the more structured 'black and white' elements and include all of the aspects that make up my definition of success. Different colors also make it easier to create emphasis, and to see how different elements overlap or relate to each other. Color really does bring concepts to life.

Create a pie chart image of what success looks like to you. Start by making a list of the things that are most important for you to have in your life. Include your personal and professional development goals, as well as your entrepreneurial business goals. Sample categories could include: personal, professional, financial, physical and spiritual needs and goals. The importance of the items in each list will give you a feel for their proportions in your pie chart. Your 'success chart' should visually answer the statement: 'I will know that I am successful when I have these things in my life, in proportions that are similar to these.'

Play with the proportions of the elements until it looks, and feels, right to you. Fine tune your graphic and keep it in a location where you can see it and refer to it whenever your daily 'to do' list seems daunting or you feel like you are moving sideways instead of forward (we've all had those days). The chart will remind you of what you are working toward. It will help keep everything in perspective. Entrepreneurs tend to make business a very large slice of their pies, which is usually necessary in the early years. Knowing that it won't always be that way — that your work won't always be all consuming — and keeping your visual of success in mind, will help you muster the motivation and the manpower needed to push on to the next level of goal achievement. (This part is also easier when you are pursuing a passion and building a business on your true Core Strengths and interests.)

Goals get you to success. They point you in the right direction and provide you with mile markers to help you gauge your progress. They let you know when you've arrived, because you have defined what success will look and feel like.

Goals should be clear, specific and measurable. Although your definition of success may be different than mine, whether or not we have reached our individual goals should be obvious through objective measurement and assessment, and not subjective evaluation. Construct your goals to include benchmarks for progress and goal attainment. Break larger goals into smaller steps to make them more easily attainable.

Including a Reason Why with each of your goals will make it easier to stay on track. State your goal and then add your reason for wanting or needing to achieve it. Napoleon Hill said it best (as he often does): 'A goal is a dream with a deadline.' Attach a timeline to the realization of your goals to keep you moving forward. We build momentum when our goal is in sight. Put your goal within reach, and within sight, and create a schedule for getting there.

Write your goals in the positive, using energetic words and phrases. Focus on what you are going to add to your life and on how you are going to build your success. Focus on your Core Strengths, your positives, and what you want your reality to become. Positive words create positive energy. The energy of your goals should make them jump off the page or the screen as you read them. They should excite you and motivate you to take action.

Be the most influential person in your life. Make sure that your goals reflect *your* true needs and desires and that they are not a reflection of what someone else feels would be right for you. Motivational Energy can only be created by focusing on *your* true strengths, talents and interests. For example, if you want to be a television producer and you opt to become an accountant because that is what someone close to you feels that you should be, your light will never be as bright as it could be, even if you become an accountant for a television station. (I'm not one of those people who feel that close is good enough.) The same goes for creating a goal that is driven primarily by a desire for great money or fame. True success goes far beyond both. If you are true to yourself, success will follow. If you are true to yourself, your Bulb will shine. You will attract what you want and more.

Goal setting is one thing. Getting to the goal is another. We cannot get to the goal until we are ready and willing to Flip the Switch and apply Active Attention to our efforts. Active Attention is the key element that separates Being the Bulb and Motivational Energy from theories and books that tell you that if you just open yourself up to the universe and wait for good things to happen they will. There is no wishing or waiting involved here. You are going to *make* things happen. Here's how.

When we Flip the Switch and apply Active Attention to our goals, we are putting our energy and intentions out into the marketplace. We are turning on our light and making it possible for people to see and feel our energy. We learned earlier that companies don't find their customers anymore. Customers find them. In order to attract the customers, (whether individuals or other companies) that we need in our business lives to be successful, we must put our energy and our message out into the marketplace, where it can be noticed, felt and acted upon. We must PUSH our energy out into the marketplace so that potential customers, mentors or other supporters can see it and PULL its message — and our products or services — towards them. We must Be Visible so that we can Be Found by them and they can then Act on the information and energy that they receive. (Remember: Attention, Interest, Desire, Action.) PUSH is when we put our energy out there for others to find. PULL is when they come looking for us or our products, with purpose (think search engines). Flipping the Switch, or Active Attention, is the fourth step in creating Motivational Energy. This is where forward momentum begins.

Flipping the Switch:
Apply Active Attention To Your Goals

The Source is only infrastructure until you consciously take action to Flip the Switch. Motivational Energy is not created until you apply Active Attention to the Source. Your Bulb will not light until you take action to channel and project your energy outward.

Applying Active Attention means 'putting it out there'. This is the point at which you are taking it public and putting your cards on the table for all to see. Flipping the Switch is the moment at which you begin acting outwardly in a manner which reflects the way that you have already begun to feel inside. You have done the work, you have assessed your strengths, you have created goals and you have created a personal branding statement that tells the world what you have to offer. This is where the marketing and the self-promotion begin. This is where you cast aside any shyness or insecurity and 'show your stuff' to the world.

We know from consumer marketing research that the package can be as important as the product. Your personal 'package' should complement your strength-based brand and be consistent with the message that you convey. Your business cards and literature should complement the image that you project. Your office environment should jive with the energy that you put into the marketplace. If you are home-based, and many new businesses are, you can still create and convey an image that is consistent with the image of your brand and your business. You do this through the way that you answer the phone or your email, with tools such as professionally presented voice mail messages, an answering service or a virtual assistant and detailed, marketing-oriented email signatures. You do this through the look and the quality of your corporate identity materials — your logo, your letterhead and your cards — whether they are presented electronically or in print.

Your professional image is also important. Your appearance and personal habits say a lot about who you are and should be consistent with the image that you are working to convey. Remember: Strong brands are clear, consistent and confident. The image that you present should be clear and strong. No waffling allowed. Every element must be consistent with the brand and its promise. You must move forward and 'put it out there' with strength and with confidence. Motivational Energy will not be created by a lackluster, half-baked effort. The turbines will not start and energy will not build unless you invest your true self into this effort. Your light will not shine unless you push your energy out there, actively and with passion. You have to want this and you need to be willing to work at it. Active Attention is what produces results and, without it, you will be left with the results of just another exercise in self-discovery and introspection: which, as we all know is nice, but not necessarily life changing.

Yes, you are dressing the part and yes, you are changing the way that you present yourself to the world, but this is not about putting on a false front. It is about letting *you* shine through and putting *your* best assets and strengths not just up front, where people can see them, but *out front*, where they *reach out to the people you want to attract and pull them toward you*. If you are projecting energy that is based on your true Core Strengths, all of these outward trappings will feel natural. Your sense of style, your behavior toward others, your professional image and work habits and even the quality of your work must be a reflection of you and your brand. They must be consistent with who you are and what you are telling the world. You will not be able to build a brand that promises quality or timely results if you are not organized, detail-minded and dedicated to deadlines. You will not be able to build a brand that is based on style, online or otherwise, if you do not care about the outward appearance of yourself or your business surroundings. You will not be able to build a confident, we-can-do-it brand if you do not stand tall, walk purposely into the room and replace the phrases "I think" and "I could" and "We might" with "I know", "I can" and "We will".

When a company creates a brand, it is creating a promise. It develops an image and identity that speaks to the target audiences and promises to fulfill a need or desire that its members have. This promise creates a set of expectations for how the brand will perform. Successful brands deliver as promised. They consistently meet the expectations that they have worked hard to create. This is what creates loyalty and brand equity. This is what makes, and keeps, a brand strong.

Personal branding takes that concept and applies it to people. When we create a personal brand for ourselves, we focus on our existing Core Strengths and capabilities — *strengths and capabilities that we already possess* — and present them to the world in a way that both creates and fulfills our 'brand promise'. That promise should build on our existing and real strengths, talents and capabilities — which is the part that some people tend to forget.

Commit yourself to self promotion. Put your brand out there, where others can see it, and not just once, but repeatedly, with strength and with clarity. Be confident in what you have to offer and present that offering to the world. If it is truly strength-based, if it is a true reflection of you, it will feel natural, look natural and be strong. Attraction Marketing combines the best of three disciplines: strength-based personal branding, target marketing and active effort and promotion. Make yourself the product. Make your brand the product. Put yourself front and center and bring your services and your business offering with you. It is all intimately related. It has to be. *That is what gives it POWER.*

We've all heard about the '30-second elevator speech' that we are all supposed to have and use — and that we've all been subjected to more than a few times in our business lives. I teach my entrepreneurial clients how to develop and present a two to three-minute pitch that is perfect for presenting to a bank, a prospective customer or an angel investor. The process requires them to think through their business concept completely and to *drill down* to the essential, need-to-know information. They learn about benefits (versus attributes, remember?) and relevant promises, messaging and Reasons Why. Then they learn to present and project not their concept, but *its benefits* to the prospect, and they learn to do so in a way that is clear, direct and compelling.

Once they have perfected this pitch — and it takes perfect pitch to get the money you need in a highly competitive market — they can use it or build on it to make a strong impression in virtually any situation. And: they do it intuitively, in a natural style and without really thinking about it. You can do the same. Think it through, write it down, restructure it, package it and learn how to present it flawlessly so that it becomes second nature. Craft your pitch, learn it, KNOW IT and then ditch it. The words and the passion should roll out naturally. They do not have to come out the same way every time, but they do have to mean the same thing. If you know and believe in your brand and its promise, your pitch will be effortless whenever and wherever you deliver it.

Other strategies for applying Active Attention and getting your brand into the marketplace include networking and publicity. Effective networking builds your contact list and creates *memorable awareness* and *positive word of mouth*. Memorable awareness is when the people you meet in a casual, non-invested situation REMEMBER YOU. You made an impression, hopefully a good one (people remember bad impressions even more easily), and they file that away in the back of their minds. Positive word of mouth is when someone who has met you elsewhere, personally worked with you, bought something from you or heard good things about you from someone whom they trust shares those positive impressions with another person (or their whole network). Today's online social networks are built on their ability to spread and build word of mouth and buzz, positive or otherwise. This is what makes them so powerful. (It's also why reputation management is so important: the information that we put into the marketplace gets passed around and often changes in the process. If you remember back to your days of playing 'telephone' with your friends — where the message you sent around the circle had totally changed by the time it got back to you — you understand how that can happen. Viral marketing is a powerful, effective and very cost effective way to promote a brand, but the filters, comments and context that friends, contacts and total strangers apply and add as they pass your information on can sometimes hurt as much as it helps. You have to 'monitor the conversation' to ensure that you brand's message remains strong and intact.)

The ultimate goal of your networking efforts should be to create memorable awareness that results in positive word of mouth and the potential pairing of two (or more) people who come together at another time to talk about you in a very positive way. The greater the number of positive 'meetings' that you facilitate — and the stronger the positive word of mouth or buzz that you create — the more likely it is that your name will come up in conversation in a positive, beneficial way. Work hard to ensure that you make a good impression, strive to build positive relationships and you will be the person that people are buzzing about. Remember, you have to Be Visible to Get Found to get referrals and to attract leads. *Be the Bulb!* and you will be the business owner, professional or executive that prospective customers and clients are drawn to.

Meeting people — networking — also provides opportunities to follow up and create memorable awareness. Following up reinforces what might have been a fairly quick or casual meeting and creates a stronger, lasting impression by providing additional information or samples of your work. You have had time to process the information that you obtained when you met your new contact and have (hopefully) created a strategy to better cultivate a relationship. Reinforcement is an important part of turning on the light. Even (especially!) a simple thank you (email is fine) or acknowledgement of the meeting provides powerful reinforcement, fosters good energy and creates positive connotations for your name in the receiver's mind. (It also puts your full contact information in front of them a second time.)

After I have met someone for the first time and determined that there is a mutual interest, need or some potential to work together, even as referral sources, I add them to my contact list. This puts them on track to receive my electronic newsletter and other periodic materials that appear just often enough to remind my contacts that I am active and visible in the marketplace, that I have valuable information to share and that I am available to work with them when they are ready. I have put myself top of mind in their minds, if only for a moment or two. That top of mind awareness, even if fleeting, brings plenty of positive connotations with it and acts as a reinforcement. They will contact me when the time is right and they are in need of the type of information or services that I have to share. I know this, because every newsletter that I distribute brings at least one new project our way. I am excited about my company and the work that we do for our clients and I know that my enthusiasm can be very contagious. That confidence shines through, when I write to them and when I see them again in person. It becomes associated with me — and my company — which is exactly how I want it to be.

Your light isn't something that you can just turn on and off. You have to be committed to the process. You must act, look and speak the part. You must Be the Brand, 24 hours a day, seven days a week. This isn't a nine-to-five proposition, this is your life — and this is your livelihood. This is who you have determined that you are, want to be and want to build on. If you are going to be true to your light and project it into the marketplace, you must do so continually and consistently. This is not about acting or manipulation. It is about putting your true self, your Core Strengths, out there. It shouldn't feel like work or seem unnatural in any way. When you apply Active Attention and Flip the Switch, you step into the role that you were born to play and begin to focus on the work that you were meant to do. You will never have a more empowering moment. You will never feel more alive. *Living your life's work and projecting your natural energy will actually make you feel more alive and empowered than ever before.*

Flipping the Switch takes courage. You are, after all, 'stepping out' and showing the real you to the world. Once you Flip the Switch and actively begin projecting, networking, promoting and *Being the Bulb*, the momentum of your Motivational Energy will carry you forward. As you begin to see results, as the people and opportunities that you hoped to attract begin to appear and come closer, your energy will build. It is as close to a self-feeding, self-fulfilling program as you can get. Confidence breeds confidence, in others and in yourself, and confidence will encourage you to stretch further, project farther, want more and risk more — all in a highly productive way. You will feel as if you have found your footing in this challenging world. When we are confident, we stand taller and walk with a greater sense of purpose. We know where we want to go and we are taking active steps to get there. It feels good and we want more of it. We feel rewarded, so we work even harder. The harder we work, the brighter our Bulb burns. The brighter our Bulb burns, the more we attract. The more we attract, the more we are encouraged and the greater the possibilities and potential we perceive. Our confidence, enthusiasm and excitement get yet another energy boost and the cycle begins again.

Success, no matter how small or simple, feeds our Motivational Energy, reinforces it and builds on it. And if you have done your work, and created a Source that is truly founded in your Core Strengths, *you will be successful*. Your light will shine. Your Bulb will burn brightly. You will begin to move forward and what you want will be attracted toward you and come closer. And like two long-separated lovers who suddenly see each other in the distance, you will begin to run faster toward your goal.

Chapter 6
Channeling and Building on Your Light

Let's take a moment to think about what we have learned so far. We know that Motivational Energy is a powerful way to market ourselves and our businesses and that when we are building and utilizing it efficiently, we are practicing Attraction Marketing. We know that Attraction Marketing is a very magnetic marketing concept which draws additional power from the exceptionally effective concepts of strength-based personal branding, target marketing and PUSH marketing strategies.

In the business world (or anywhere, for that matter), you get what you ask for. You also get back what you believe in and actively project, especially when you do it with energy and enthusiasm. The reverse is also true. You rarely get what you don't ask for and few people will have confidence in you if you do not have confidence in yourself. In order to attract the success that you want to create and enjoy as an entrepreneur, you must be confident in yourself and your strengths. You must project a clear, consistent brand that conveys the value and benefit of those strengths to the people who can help you become successful, whether they are customers, mentors, investors or partners.

Attraction Marketing works for entrepreneurs in any field and for businesses of any size. You can use strength-based assessment, branding and message development to choose your business, choose your customers and choose how you will succeed. Few business strategies are as fully empowering or as successful.

An Attraction Marketing-based strategy will work for you whether your business is new or established, growing, struggling or expanding rapidly. Are you a non-entrepreneur working for someone else right now? Effectively harnessing and projecting Motivational Energy can help you attract the career success that you want by making you a more valued and recognized employee. Your efforts and contributions will never go unnoticed again.

The process to create and project Motivational Energy is much like the process that must take place before the bulb in a lamp will light. There must be a Power Source, which is cultivated and harnessed. This power comes from your Core Strengths, which are the Source of your Motivational Energy. There must be Conduit to guide the energy, in the form of goals and intentions, and there must be a Switch, where you apply Active Attention and begin projecting your energy outward. Remember: It is all only infrastructure until you Flip the Switch and convert it into Motivational Energy. Action — Active Attention and effort — is what makes the difference.

As your Motivational Energy makes its way out into the marketplace, you must guide it — to ensure that it is efficiently projected in the proper direction. Think about how the conduit in the walls of your home or office guide power from the source (external) to the switch (in the room) and how additional conduit — a cord and a plug — then take the active energy directly to the lamp (or other target). In Attraction Marketing, this second set of Conduit is comprised of the strategies that you put into place and follow to achieve your goals. When your energy is directed carefully and consistently, and remains strong and true, your Bulb will light and you will begin to attract what you want and need to be successful.

Need to put it into a stronger business framework? Think of the assessment and identification of your Core Strengths as a business plan that will guide your efforts. The first set of Conduit represents the Strategic Plan, the Mission Statement and the Goals that you will implement to move your business forward. The second set of Conduit represents those strategies at work. You have Flipped the Switch and are applying Active Attention. The second set of Conduit ensures that you stay on track, toward your goals, much as the Strategy section of your business plan is designed to help you do.

The Importance of Staying on Target

You have developed goals and strategies, Flipped the Switch and are now actively projecting your Motivational Energy outward. Targeting ensures that you remain on goal, and that your energy is being directed into the marketplace in the most efficient way possible.

You are in the preparation phase until the point at which you Flip the Switch and begin to apply Active Attention. You assess and identify your Core Strengths and create a power Source. The goals that you develop in this phase identify a destination that will guide your efforts. The strategies that you devise will create the Conduit that will move your energy forward in a productive direction and toward the realization of your goals. The excitement, motivation and sense of purpose that you begin to feel during this process will help build your Motivational Energy and propel you and it toward the point where you are ready to apply Active Attention and push your energy out into the marketplace, where others can visibly see it, and begin to feel it.

Once you begin applying Active Attention, you are *projecting*. That same excitement, motivation and sense of purpose will keep your Motivational Energy moving outward, especially as you begin to see results. Results and feedback act as reinforcement — reinforcement in the form of positive input or actions, opportunities and events that begin to occur and signal to you that *you are on track*. As your energy moves outward, your Bulb will begin to glow. As positive results and reinforcement come back to you, it will begin to shine. You will realize that you are on the right path and that your efforts are well directed. You will begin to see the potential of what you are doing. You will begin to feel that you are moving forward, even if only slightly, toward where you want to be. You will realize that you can do this, that you are doing it, and that you are capable of doing even more. You will feel movement and the beginnings of momentum.

You will feel confident.

Confidence is what will truly light your bulb and cause it to shine at it brightest. Confidence is what creates the magnetic pull that brings others towards you and into your orbit, like moths to a flame or a light. Confidence is what encourages you to rev up the engines and put more fuel into the process to push — and project — more Motivational Energy into the marketplace. Your light is shining. You are *Being the Bulb*. You are confident and strong and feel capable. It is a very empowering feeling.

The step from preparing to projecting is a big one. It takes courage to Flip the Switch, courage that comes from feeling prepared and ready to take on the world. Investing the time and effort it takes to do the preparation will get you there. Creating a plan will make you feel ready. Having that plan in hand will give you the courage you need to take the first step, with purpose, and with a clear destination in mind. Following your plan and staying on strategy will keep your energy moving forward in the most efficient way possible, toward your goals. This is called *targeting*. It is represented by the second set of Conduit, the one that leads directly to the bulb. Effectively targeting the energy that you create is a critical part of the process of *Being the Bulb*.

Without targeting, your Motivational Energy would be projected out into the marketplace without focus or direction (or a clear result). You would feel happier and more motivated because you are focused on our Core Strengths, but you would be projecting energy without a sense of purpose. Think about the comparison of a streetlight and a flashlight again. A streetlight casts a very general light that is beneficial, but not very focused or task-specific. A flashlight is directional and helps you find your way. It is focused, direct and sheds light in highly specific areas. You point it toward where you want to go and it will help you get there safely. You shine it into a dimly lit area or nook and it will help you see better. You point it under or behind something and it can help you find what you are looking for. The light of the flashlight is very focused. It is a tool that is very results oriented.

Like the light that is produced by the streetlight, any light that you create is helpful, but can be diffused by generality. Unless you target your Motivational Energy, it will not be focused on your goals. The same holds true in advertising, where limited dollars and resources are applied carefully to target the highest potential prospects. Target marketing enables limited resources to be utilized more efficiently. Instead of advertising to the world, we advertise to the people who are most likely to become our customers and buy our products. Instead of talking to everyone, we speak to the people who are mostly likely to listen to and like what we have to say. Instead of trying to be all things to all people, we focus our message (branding) and speak to our prospects in a voice (messaging) that reaches them in an environment and in a way (media) that is comfortable and familiar to them, and that communicates the benefits of doing business with our company (advertising). Targeting is implicit in every step of that equation. We focus on strengths to create a brand; we develop a message that focuses on the key benefits that we have to offer; we develop a media (online or otherwise) plan that utilizes vehicles and tools that research has told us our prospects favor; and we specifically apply resources (financial, time and human) to those choices and strategies to achieve the levels of reach and frequency that we need to create Attention, Interest, Desire and Action.

See how it's all coming together?

Staying on target is very important to *Being the Bulb* and in Part IV I will provide you with guidelines for keeping your Motivational Energy — and your message — focused and on track. But first, I am going to go to the heart of the matter and provide you with powerful strategies for promoting yourself and your business. These strategies will help you create a context for later chapters on targeting, gatekeeping and (second-stage) growth strategies. Active promotion is the conduit that guides your energy outward and in a focused direction. You can compare it to the section on implementation strategies in your business plan. It is a process that I call *Getting to the Goal*.

Be The Bulb!

Part III: Putting It To Work: Powerful Strategies To Promote You and Your Company

Chapter 7
Creating A Powerful Brand That Shines Brightly

Creating energy from inner strengths is one thing. Knowing how to direct and fully utilize your new-found energy is another. You've read about the concept of Attraction Marketing and how it can help you create success for yourself and your business. You've learned how Motivational Energy is created and compounded. Now I am going to explain how you can put what you have read and learned to work to identify, grasp and even create the opportunities that you need to successfully reach your goals.

Effectively projecting Motivational Energy into the marketplace is all about directing your efforts at the right audience and putting your best foot forward. It is about knowing yourself and your business well enough to be able to focus on real, inherent strengths and not just strengths that you see being marketed successfully by others. It is about knowing your target market well enough to know what they need and want to buy, and what they need and want to hear about it. It is about creating entrepreneurial success by matching your offering to those needs and your message to the needs of both. It is entrepreneurial, success-oriented matchmaking at its finest!

The same principles and concepts can be used to market yourself or your company. Strength-based branding and benefit-focused messaging strategies can be put to work effectively in any marketing scenario. You must PUSH your message out into the marketplace and make it Visible so that it can Be Found by the people who can help you succeed. They, in turn, will be ATTRACTED (Attention) to your energy and your message by its relevance (Interest), will PULL (Desire) what they need from it, and will find themselves drawn to you and your company in doing so (Action).

And all of this will likely take place without you meeting them in person or talking to them by phone or email.

So much has changed and so much is possible. The Internet has rewritten many of the rules of marketing and has changed the way that companies do business. The size of the market has changed and selling opportunities have grown exponentially. Every company now has the potential to become a global company with global reach. Geography is no longer a limitation. The potential to communicate with a larger, more diverse audience has increased dramatically. The cost of media no longer creates insurmountable barriers to entry for new and still-small businesses. Success (and the potential to succeed) is no longer defined by mere size or resources. Speed, innovation and creativity have become much more important. The way that people obtain information on products and services has changed, as have the ways that they make buying decisions and purchases. New industries have been built around information finding, sorting and sharing. In a world where everyone can have a website, it seems like just about everyone does. The sheer volume of information and choices is staggering in such a market without boundaries. How can a company stand out in a marketplace where access to information on just about any topic is limited only by a person's ability to come up with new and creative Google combinations and search phrases?

Prospecting, positive word of mouth, testimonials and referrals have never been more important, as a greater percentage of your potential customers become members of an 'invisible audience' that you may never meet in person or communicate with directly. Potential customers who knew nothing about you or your company this morning can learn a lot about both in very little time, by searching articles and reviews, mentions and links and potentially even talking to some of your current or former customers. In today's online marketplace, you have little control over what is said or shared about you and your brand, but you do have the ability to monitor and influence the conversations that take place. Monitoring a brand has literally become an ongoing process. It surely has become a necessary one.

Attraction marketing projects your message into the marketplace in order to attract back what you need or want. Social networking takes place when people connect with each other online and then SHARE or PUSH information around their extended network of contacts. Viral marketing occurs when they share or push product or other *marketing-related* information to others in their networks. Consider the potential that social networking holds for exponential information movement and, potentially, sales. Think about how far your message can travel once you have projected it into the marketplace. Think about the influence that positive, pass-along testimonials and viral marketing can have in certain peer groups. Think about what it can do for your brand.

But first it has to BE FOUND.

A Brand That Breathes

Products that meet specific needs and that are properly positioned and promoted will be successful. The same rule applies to people. Your personal brand should be a reflection of who you are, your Core Strengths and the value-adding benefits that your offering provides. Ditto for your company and its products. Create a positioning statement built on your Core Strengths, a message with a compelling Promise and a Reason Why that supports that position, and then project that message toward potential customers who have a related need or share an interest in your offering. A product (and remember, people are also products) with an authentic customer focus is a product that fulfills a need, satisfies a desire or solves a problem for a prospective customer. Strength-based branding matches inherent strengths and benefits with parallel marketplace demand. It is authentic, organic and holistic because it deals with the realities of both sides of the marketing equation. This is what makes it successful. It puts your best foot forward to enable you to find your strongest natural footing. I call it Motivational Energy for two primary reasons: 1) It motivates you, as the 'brand manager' to work harder, push further and shine brighter than you have ever done before; and 2) It motivates prospective customers to PULL themselves toward you and your company and add their energy (and their purchases or other support) to your light, thereby feeding and building on it. Motivational Energy is self-created and self-feeding AND it is compounded by the energy, input and resources of others. Once your light begins to glow, once your Bulb begins to shine, you will attract what you need to grow stronger. You will create momentum and momentum will keep your bulb burning brightly, even when you are not actively working to build it. We will learn more about this in the chapter on evolution and inertia. For now, what is important to remember is this: Success feeds your light. Even one prospect inquiry, sale or contract will add energy to your efforts. Your confidence will grow, your light will shine brighter and you will attract others to your energy. This is why it is so important to invest time in message strategy. If you 'get it right' right out of the gate — as your Motivational Energy hits the marketplace — you are likely to see faster results. Messages that resonate work — and they resonate because they are on target AND because they are targeted to reach prospects in their preferred environments. *It is all about them, not you. Really.*

If you have developed a business plan at some point in your career (or even just learned about doing so in school or through business center counseling), you know that there are generally accepted outlines for content and structure. There is, however, no such thing as a 'one size fits all' business plan format that fits every type of business or concept. There are essential elements that should be included, such as detailed descriptions of your proposed product or service and your intended customer, the current and potential market, marketing and sales strategies, detailed financials (including expected sales, expenses, cash flow, profitability and funding needs) and related timeframes for the realization of each of your goals. I am not going to take you through the steps of developing a business plan. There are untold resources available to help you do this and dozens of books that dive into the subject in detail. (You can also obtain free advice and counseling from business experts through the SBA's national network of Small Business Development Centers (SBDC). Learn more at www.sba.gov/sbdc.)

I am going to provide you with an understanding of what it takes to harness the Motivational Energy that you have created and convert it into a targeted, relevant message that will resonate with the people who can help bring success into your life. Your message and your energy are the light that you project when you are *Being the Bulb*. Cultivating that light requires more of a message strategy than a business development strategy, but it does require a plan.

As a graduate student at Northwestern University, I had the opportunity to learn from one of the greatest advertising and marketing experts in the world: Don Schultz, who is widely considered to be the 'father of integrated marketing'. In his first book, *Essentials of Advertising Strategy* (Crain Books, 1981), Schultz promotes a multi-point creative strategy development process that shares similarities with the outline of a basic business plan. Don't be put off by the publication date. The principles of the outline are timeless and the process — and its result — are still far more effective than any communications strategy outline that I have come across since. The process that Schultz outlines is designed to develop a message that is 'on target' and that addresses the need, or the marketing problem, at hand. Schultz's process begins by addressing the problem or issue by 1) Stating the Key Fact and 2) Describing the Problem that Marketing Can Solve. The process to develop a Creative Strategy that addresses this problem then goes on to:

1) Define the Product or Service (both in reality and as perceived);

2) Define the Target Audience (by geography, demographics, psychographics, media patterns and buying/usage patterns);

3) Describe the Principal Competition;

4) Describe the Competitive Consumer Benefit;

5) Provide a Reason Why;

6) Develop a Target Market Incentive Statement;

7) Address the Tone of the Message; and

8) State the Communication Objective (what is the main point of the message and what is the desired action that should be taken by the recipient?).

The purpose of presenting this outline is not to teach you how to develop a winning creative strategy, although this process will definitely increase the odds that you'll come up with a winner. The real gem is the *thought process* that Schultz's outline promotes. If you take away two key pieces of information from this entire discussion on marketing, you will never go wrong (and you will be light years ahead of most of your competition): 1) understand the difference between benefits and attributes; and 2) know that you need to have a compelling 'reason why' for any message, in any situation. Let's tackle them one at a time.

You read about the difference between benefits and attributes in an earlier chapter. Your ability to focus on the needs of a prospect, and to be able to communicate a message that directly appeals to those needs in language that he or she can relate to and understand, is the most fundamental component of your potential communication and sales success. Prospect empathy and understanding is a key element of successful targeting and it is essential to effectively projecting Motivational Energy. Remember, Attraction Marketing is founded in the purest targeting and branding concepts and is strength based. When you can translate your Core Strengths into Competitive Consumer Benefits that meet needs, fulfill desires and solve problems for your target audience, you will be shining at your very brightest. You will create charismatic, magnetic message energy that draws your targets toward your light and fuels it by their closeness and involvement. The stronger your brand and its message and the more compelling your Reason Why, the faster and closer your prospects will pull themselves toward your light, and your company and its products.

What makes a good message strategy? Your brand's message must convey a compelling benefit that fulfills a need or solves a problem that your target audience finds themselves faced with. If your brand is offering a solution, it should be a solution that is perceived as practical, desirable and believable. If it is describing the bundle of services or strengths that you have to offer, they must be perceived as offering tangible results and being value-adding. Someone has to want, need or desire what you are offering if you are going to be successful. More importantly, they have to *know* that they want, need or desire your product. A great message strategy sets up a situation or need, makes a promise, includes a believable Reason Why and asks for the sale — typically in very few words or through a single compelling image. Great advertising and media messages are a challenge to create and the most memorable ones are often stunning in their simplicity ('Just do it!') Those of us in the advertising industry know that it only looks easy. An enormous amount of research and thought has to go into the process.

Your message statement must be tied to your brand. You learned about positioning (creating an identity for your product that claims a piece of marketspace in the prospect's mind) and the need to create a Competitive Consumer Benefit, a Unique Selling Proposition or a Value Proposition (which are three marketing-speak terms for virtually the same thing). Your positioning statement (how you want the prospect to perceive and categorize your product) sets the stage for your Competitive Consumer Benefit (which, hopefully, claims the category). Your Competitive Consumer Benefit should be unique enough — and brand-specific enough — that no other advertiser can easily make the same claim. It should distinguish your brand in some relative, discernible and value-adding way to make the association between your brand and the promise strong and clear. If your brand's name can be easily replaced with the name of another person or product in the message statement, your message (and its promise) are too broadly stated. Drill down and focus on you or your product's strengths and present them in a way which is relevant to the prospect's needs but also unique to the marketplace. Support your Competitive Consumer Benefit with a strong Reason Why and and add an even stronger call to action. This is what makes a message compelling (relevance, uniqueness, believability and a sense of urgency). Then project your message and the energy that it contains into the marketplace and directly at your target audience — in words, images, sounds and actions, via face to face marketing and through word of mouth, both online and off. Stay on message, on strategy and on target. Consistency and frequency build strong brands.

I have utilized this basic strategic planning process or some variation of it to make critical decisions and create innovative messages and strategies throughout my 30-year career, for both myself and my clients. It is one of the most effective tools that I have in my consulting and entrepreneurial arsenals. When I realized how I had been creating Motivational Energy over the years without really thinking about it, I gave it a name and began systematically building and projecting my energy toward my personal and professional goals through a process that I now call Attraction Marketing.

My visibility, my business, my light *and my success* grew exponentially. There really was no limit to how far my company could have grown, other than my personal desire to keep my ventures closely held. I am a successful serial *lifestyle* entrepreneur who values a high quality of life and a good income over sheer volume or size. I have absolutely no doubt that I could have taken my marketing company multi-national years ago, had I chosen to. For me, success has never been about sheer size.

A message strategy that focuses on your Core Strengths and the benefits that they provide will attract prospective customers who place value on that offering. Every business needs to have a clear understanding of who their Ideal Customer is. An Ideal Customer is a prospect who has a clear need or desire for your offer AND has the incentive, the ability and the resources to act on it.

Attraction Marketing first identifies an Ideal Customer as someone who is inclined to be open to your energy and message and then creates a strategy to attract their attention and interest. As you have learned, successful communicating and selling involves four elements: Attention, Interest, Desire and Action. It is easier to capture the attention of people who are already inclined to be interested in you and your offering. It will always be easier to create awareness among people who have needs and desires that are well-matched to your brand and its benefit offering. It is more likely that you will capture the interest of prospects who are attracted to the strength and the similarity of your energy with their own energy and needs, and who become aware of this synergy in an environment in which they feel comfortable. If your message is clear, concise and on target, it is likely that their interest will evolve into Desire, which is the prelude to Action. You want them to want you and your products. You want them to want you and your brand. You want them to be drawn to your light and to move toward it. You need to make it as easy as possible for this to happen.

A true Ideal Customer fits a profile that complements your brand and its offering AND has the access, the resources and the inclination to actively pursue, purchase and pay for your product. Think about that. An Ideal Customer doesn't just fit the profile, he or she also has the ability, and the willingness, to put their money where their mouth is, so to speak. They are active in the marketplace, searching for a product solution and are a ready, willing and able buyer. Your greatest potential for sales success lies with these prospects.

To know them is to sell them. Invest time identifying, describing and getting to know your Ideal Customers. Describe him, her or them in detailed words and in demographic categories such as age, sex, education, household income, marital status, home ownership and more. Where do these prospects live (geographically), how do they live (type of housing) and who do they live with (marital and family status), what do they do for a living (job or profession) and how do they make buying decisions? Describe their general perspective and purchasing behavior (psychographics). Are they early adopters, followers or late bloomers? Savers or spenders? Brand conscious buyers or savvy shoppers? What other brands are they using now and why? Research and understand their media habits. What media do they use, online and off? How do they obtain their information (news, product, entertainment, etc.) and share it? How do they interact with others? Are they new media users or traditionalists? Are they tuned into trends or do they tend toward the safe and established? What are their priorities and drivers? What is important to them and why? These are only a sampling of the questions that you should ask and answer to create a detailed profile of the Ideal Customers who were born to be attracted to your brand. Get to know them, intimately. They are your Target Audience.

Your Ideal Customer may be your best sales target, but there are other key audiences that you must also want to shine your light on. These are people who are in a position to help you succeed, by spreading the word about your business, making referrals, leading you to needed financing, introducing you to contacts you should know, mentoring your business or otherwise facilitating your efforts. They could be your future business partners or employees, professional service providers, peer group members or sought-after members of the media or government. Do not limit your visibility by only reaching out to people whom you believe that you can sell things to. Also invest your energy toward attracting the attention of those who can add fuel to your efforts and help your light shine even more brightly.

Be The Bulb!

Chapter 8
Putting Your Brand in the Spotlight

Light is a visual experience. It has to be seen to be known, even if only faintly. Humans are drawn to the promise of light. It is in our nature. A light in the distance, a burning ember, the sparkle of a brilliant diamond, the faraway glow of the sun rising over the horizon or setting below it, all of these hold the promise of a stronger, more brilliant light — especially as we draw closer, or look within.

Be the Bulb! and put the promise of your brand and its offering on the radar of your Ideal Customers. Put your energy and your message in places that they frequent, do business and can be found on a regular basis. Set the stage, choose your audience carefully, script your message to appeal to your Ideal Customers and your actions to reach out to them and your efforts will shine a spotlight on your company.

Cross the path of their awareness and capture their attention. Create interest. Encourage desire. Incite action. Always. When you are true to your Core Strengths, your light will shine brightly. When you put that light directly in the path of your Ideal Customer, you will be actively targeting — and attracting — the people you need in your life to be successful.

The strategies that I am about to discuss can help you achieve two key elements of your marketing goals: creating memorable awareness for your brand and providing powerful reinforcement that builds brand strength and momentum. Very few marketing tools are only useful in one situation or another. There are no precise promotional prescriptions, only general truths that you can apply to your specific needs and goals. The art of marketing — and it is an art, no question about it — is to determine the most efficient and effective strategy to achieve a highly specific set of marketing goals. (The art comes in both the goal identification and the strategy, or tool, development.) This does not mean utilizing every possible tool in the tool box. This does not mean blindly doing what others are doing because it is trendy, or popular, or even successful. This is about implementing *the right strategy for you and your brand*. Just as your Core Strengths are reflected and supported in the personal and product brands that you have created, your marketing strategy must be a true reflection of those same strengths, their competitive benefits, a compelling promise that they make and a clear Reason Why. Begin with a strong set of specific marketing goals for communicating strengths and their benefits and you are well on your way to determining HOW to achieve them. If you have conducted a comprehensive Situation Analysis, developed a detailed Target Audience statement that identifies and describes your Ideal Customer and stated clear Goals and Objectives for the Problem That Marketing Can Solve, you will be well-armed to develop a marketing strategy that will help you achieve those goals by Putting Your Light in the Path of Your Ideal Customers.

Cross the path of their awareness with a compelling, benefit-driven message and you will capture their attention. Attention is an opportunity to create Interest, Desire and Action. Awareness, and attention, must be your goal.

I have built my marketing and public relations firm on the concept of planting a seed and then cultivating it carefully to maturity. Over the years, I have assembled a list of prospects, clients and contacts that I add to regularly, and with great thought. It is no mere laundry list of names and email addresses. My contact lists includes only those people whom I truly believe can benefit from working with me in some capacity.

I have an electronic newsletter that I send to these contacts on a bi-monthly basis that is filled with information that recipients can use in some way: marketing advice and trends, just-released, cutting edge books to read, insights on the WHY behind smart marketing and PR strategies, as well advice that guides the HOW. My newsletters keep contacts up to date on what we're up to as a company, project-wise, but they do not sell in any heavy handed way. (They don't have to. The mentions of our client and project successes are proof enough of what we can do.) I regularly have recipients who tell me that they enjoy my newsletters because they learn from them. I have heard the same about my blog. My newsletter has a very high readership rate, a low bounce rate and a high click-through rate to my website. This tells me that I am offering something of value to the people who receive it. That has always been my goal: to cultivate a relationship that gets — and keeps me — on their radar.

I have also invested a great deal of time in networking and in being in the right place to invite business opportunities my way. When I was working to build my firm's reputation in economic development nearly 20 years ago, I made it a point to be at every event that was related to the topic in my region. The visibility and the contacts that I created through that effort proved to be priceless and resulted in countless referrals to related business (and still do). Many of those early relationships continue to this day.

I made a conscious effort to place myself in the path of people who could help me grow my business. My light was only just beginning to shine back in 1988 when I founded my firm. Fortunately (and I do attribute this to my marketing education and to my early career experience in the advertising industry), I realized early that, the more that I focused my efforts and energy on one key area — in this case, economic development and community marketing — the more rapidly my reputation would grow. I became an expert in my field, as opposed to just another local marketing and PR firm that 'did everything' and my name and my company's name became synonymous with economic development marketing in my region. We were invited to bid on major projects and, as we successfully completed that work, we always received referrals for new business. Our reputation grew based on the quality of our work, our expanding network and my insistence on being the number-one firm in one niche of a highly competitive industry.

Nearly ninety percent of my company's new business comes from referrals by satisfied customers and it has been that way for many years. That is a huge testimonial to the quality and value of our services and our work, and it puts us in the interesting position of being a marketing company that doesn't have to do very much marketing. Our light is strong and it continues to shine brightly two decades later (we celebrated our twentieth anniversary as a firm in 2008). My visibility as a consultant, a speaker and now also as an author, creates awareness and brings attention our way, from both our long-term clients and new contacts. Our newsletter is a beacon that directs our light (both my brand and my company's brand) at the people who matter to us most. It keeps us top of mind with this important audience (and yes, most of them fall directly into our Ideal Customer category) and provides them with (free) expert advice that they can put to work immediately if they choose to. Here's the best part: I have never put out a newsletter that did not result in at least one piece of new business. Never, not once, in the nearly ten years that it has existed (we began our newsletter in 1998 and it went fully electronic in 2006). No kidding.

Here's what you should take away from my experience: Find and cultivate the people who can help you grow your business and then put your light in the path of their awareness on a regular basis to 1) get their attention; 2) provide them with something of value to keep it; and 3) build and maintain a relationship that provides value to both sides. Continuously work to strengthen and build on these relationships through communication, product quality and service. Don't just promote the brand, Be the Brand. Always deliver more than you promise and be willing to add value in ways that don't always put money in your pocket. Build the Relationship. I want my clients to see me as a partner in their success, not just as a vendor *and I want to be able to say the same of them*. Remember science class and that lecture on mutually beneficial symbiotic relationships? That's what a good business relationship should do: provide something beneficial, and of value, to both parties.

Be the Bulb! and your symbiotic relationships will multiply exponentially. That has been my experience, without question.

Image is also very important in branding and marketing. Building awareness for yourself and your company begins with the image that you develop, project and associate with your brand. This includes corporate identity standards (font, color, usage) and logos for company and product brands, and the appearance, presentation and quality of personal and identity elements for personal brands.

Your company or product logo should be simple, clean and to the point. It should convey or complement the core benefit of your brand in a relative way and be easily identifiable and distinctive. Strong logos have crisp, clear elements, clean lines and relatively simple fonts that work well in any color environment (black and white or color), online and off. Never overdo this element of your marketing, which is an execution of your branding strategy, not a strategy in itself. Less *is* more, really. Keep it simple, uncluttered and iconic, like Apple, and strive to create a brand image that one day could similarly convey a powerful, emotional message that doesn't require a company name or any other words to be understood.

Image — the way that you present yourself to the people you meet — is critically important to personal brands. How you dress, accessorize, conduct yourself and present your office, your communications and your work are all part of the image that potential contacts and customers evaluate you by. All of these elements should be consistent with your brand strategy. A professional, top-drawer brand requires an equally top-drawer, five-star image. A casual, comfortable brand can accommodate a more casual, comfortable approach in your image and marketing, although professionalism is always important. In either case, it is critical to convey confidence. (If you appear confident, the world will have confidence in you.) Walk and enter a room with purpose, head held high, making eye contact and reaching out to shake hands with people at the moment that you greet or meet them. Introduce yourself briefly and then listen as they do the same. Ask a question and *engage* them in the moment to make it more of an experience than a greeting. They will remember your outreach and your interest, and they will remember *you*.

Remember, *Being the Bulb* is about lighting up a room that you enter with your dynamic, engaging presence. Forget the room as you enter and focus on the people whom you meet. Focused attention makes your light shine and attracts others toward you (or at least makes them very receptive to your approach). It is the human ingredient that those infamous 'business card bombers' ignore as they hit and run a room to 'meet' as many people as possible in the shortest amount of time — and the reason that so many of their business cards end up in wastebaskets.

The quality of your work (or product) and the level of the service that you provide to your customers must also deliver on your brand promise. Both should ALWAYS be exceptional, regardless of how casual your brand may appear to be on the surface. Providing extraordinary customer or client service and doing work that exceeds the expectations of the people and companies that you work with will always set you apart from the competition. Sadly, many companies over promise and under deliver in today's marketplace. This provides a real market opportunity for those companies that are willing to really do the work and provide a great product delivered with a smile and supported by great service. Be the brand that meets and exceeds expectations (and promises) and you will quickly distinguish yourself in the marketplace. Deliver a positive, fulfilling purchase experience and your customers will come back for more. They will tell others about their positive experience and your business will grow. Attention and service are very value adding and many customers are willing to pay more to obtain both. This could also enable you to charge more for your products and services (or introduce a higher-priced brand extension) once you have established a reputation for exceptional service in your category.

Your image should be consistently presented every time that you communicate with a customer or prospect. 'Snail mail' may be on the decline, but there will always be a need for well-designed corporate identity materials such as letterhead (printed or electronic), envelopes, business cards and email signature. Pay to have your materials professionally designed. These are the elements that will be most associated with you and your brand on a day-to-day basis. Make sure that every impression is a good one. Your business card should include your name, phone number(s), email address and website at minimum. Most essential communication takes places by email these days and street addresses have become optional. In many circles, they make a card look dated. Using a vertical card format is more forgiving than it used to be. Few people use a Rolodex to hold their cards anymore. The most important criteria? Make sure that your card is legible. Design is important, but readability is key. Fonts that are too small or reversed on a background that does not provide enough contrast are hard to read, in any light, and annoying. Your card will be the cue that people use to remember and contact you with. Make it easy to work with, just like you.

Your email signature should convey your brand and be presented in a way which is consistent with its image. Include your name, company name, phone number, a link to your website and (potentially) a brief branding statement or tagline (make sure it is benefit focused!). My email signature includes a link to my blog and, sometimes, a link to information on a hot project that I am working on. I also have a version that includes an invitation to connect through one of the social networking sites that I am active on. Having multiple email signature blocks to choose from is a good strategy (Outlook makes this easy). Often, I customize one of my existing templates to send a link to something especially relative to a contact. The point is: use every email as the branding opportunity that it is and customize it, if necessary, to fit the contact.

Printed collaterals don't play quite a starring role as they used to in business marketing, but they are still essential to making a good first meeting or follow up impression. In today's marketplace, my company designs collaterals — which includes elements such as brochures of all sizes and direct mail pieces of every shape and kind — to be both printed and sent electronically by our clients. Invest in having high quality, attractive materials designed and written by professionals that support your branding and marketing strategies and then print only enough to take you through the first six months of your marketing program. (Yes, I know, printing twice as many only costs a few dollars more, but think of the ecological impact when you end up throwing them away because they have become outdated before you used them all.) Today's printing technologies have made four-color printing much more affordable, especially for short runs. This makes it much more practical to update and reprint pieces to reflect changes in your company, its products, the marketplace or the competition.

Use your collaterals in this one-two punch manner. When you meet someone for the first time, perhaps at a networking event, exchange cards and your best version of your 'elevator speech' (a 30-second, carefully crafted description of what you do, as a customer-focused benefit statement). Be sure to *engage* them by asking a question about what they do, *listening*, and then acknowledging their response with a follow-up comment. Your interest will make a positive impression. When you return to your office, email your new contact a personalized follow-up note and the electronic file of your current brochure or other collateral. Your email should acknowledge the meeting, thank the contact for their time and offer a reason for them to want to get to know more about you and your company. Offer a competitive advantage, a solution to a problem or need that they mentioned while chatting with you (always refer to something that they said during your meeting, no matter how brief the interaction may have been) or some other benefit that is related to the setting in which you met them. This could be an article or some other information that you referred to during your conversation. (Remember, following up is a lost art these days. Follow up promptly and with style and you *will* be remembered.) And: environment and context are very important. Frame your email as a follow up to a stated need or interest and not as a stone-cold sales pitch by creating commonality and a sense of shared space. Reference how you met (where or through whom) to reinforce that first contact.

After you have sent off your email, put together a package of printed materials and send them off to your new contact, along with a brief cover letter. Add a suggestion for a way in which you could do business together or help each other in some way. This is not redundant. This is reinforcement. It indicates that you have a true interest in working with them and demonstrates continued follow up. By the time they receive your envelope and go through it, they will have interacted with you and your brand a minimum of three times (and potentially more if they followed up on your email with a phone call of their own). Every interaction reminds them of you and your meeting. Every interaction reinforces you and your brand. This is why it is so important that all of your collaterals (electronic and printed) reflect your true strengths and your true brand. They will carry the weight of your follow-up efforts and reinforce the positive impression that you worked so hard to make when you met your new contact face to face.

Keep the following four steps in mind as you read about different strategies and tools for reaching out to prospects and projecting your message into the marketplace. I have this short list printed on a piece of paper that I keep near my computer and my headset — the two tools that I utilize to do the bulk of my communicating. In any selling or prospecting situation, a series of steps must take place if you are going to be successful in creating and maintaining productive long-term relationships that develop from turning new contacts into new customers:

1) Make yourself visible;

2) Plant the idea;

3) Ask for the sale;

4) Provide exceptional follow up and service. Always.

You have to Be Visible to Get Found. You made yourself visible when you invested the effort to meet and greet your new contact at the event, or when you responded in a professional and engaging manner when he or she came up to shake your hand. You built on that visibility by actively following up by email and providing more information. You got their attention and created some level of awareness.

Now plant the idea. Meeting someone is not enough. Strive to create a lasting, positive impression that get them thinking about how they could work with you to fulfill a need or desire that they have or to solve a problem that they are dealing with. Create a context for building a new and productive relationship that is focused on their immediate (or an upcoming) need or issue. Then reinforce this context by using your follow up opportunity to make suggestions (solicited or otherwise) that provide practical, objective advice *and* underline the benefit of knowing and working with you and your company.

Ask for the sale, always, by asking for an opportunity to meet (or talk) with the contact again to discuss their specific situation and needs in a more business-focused setting. Use your judgment, based on the nature of your business and its product. Only you can decide whether the situation requires more information (and the relationship more nurturing), or if the time is right for a detailed proposal or price quote. The key is to include a call to action, which asks for such an opportunity, or presents the information needed to close a deal. Remember: Attention, Interest, Desire, and then Action. You have their attention. Ask them to confirm their interest — or build on it — and then go one step further, by participating in a face to face meeting or a phone call, by requesting additional information or by agreeing to add their name to your newsletter list. Always help your contact actively move toward the next step.

Once you have been given an opportunity to serve them in some way, either by following up with additional information, a proposal, a referral or (in the best case scenario) an assignment or sale, make sure that you do so in a way which delivers a highly positive, relationship-building experience. Provide extraordinary service that reinforces their purchase decision and you are well on your way to building a long-term customer relationship. Performance — service — will also reinforce the relationship and continue to 'sell' on your behalf, even when you are not actively cultivating the account. *Being the Bulb* and attracting energy is not enough. You must also meet the needs of the people whom you attract in some way, so that they stay aware and connected to you. Every satisfied customer and well-served contact will make your light shine brighter, and their growing numbers will attract still others to you. Creating satisfied, happy customers feeds your light, and theirs, and the process becomes beneficially cyclical. Every time that you successfully complete the cycle — Be Visible, Plant the Idea, Ask for the Sale and Provide Exceptional Service — your light will become stronger. It is a self-feeding, self-fulfilling process that is very powerful.

Applying Active Attention — proactively projecting your message and your Motivational Energy into the marketplace — is the implementation phase of Attraction Marketing. You Flipped the Switch and are actively promoting yourself (or your company and its products) through a strategic effort that is designed to put your light into the path of the people who can help you succeed. You now know who they are and you are actively working to catch their attention with your light.

Advertising is one way to reach out to prospects and to shine your light at an audience that you cannot reach directly. Every ad that you put into the marketplace should be a true execution of your message strategy. Advertising that is *on message* and *on target* (directed at the desired prospects) will help you achieve your objectives. Traditional media platforms that promote you or your products include print (newspapers and magazines), broadcast (radio and television, whether cable, satellite or 'free'), direct mail and outdoor (billboards, vehicle signing, balloons, skywriting, the works). Media planning and buying is an art and it is best to get the help of a professional when you are ready to begin spending money on ad placement. Buying every advertising opportunity or 'deal' that comes along (no matter how good it may sound) is not going to accomplish anything except use up your resources quickly. Placing an ad in your favorite magazine or on your favorite radio or cable television show is not going to reach your target audience unless your media habits happen to match the media profile of your target audience. Online advertising and media selection requires a very different approach and I will cover it separately in an upcoming section on new media.

Many people think of effective publicity, or public relations (PR), as 'free advertising' and, in a way, it is. Public relations utilizes strategies that garner attention and create positive awareness for your brand or your company and its products. Publicists make their living working to get inches of favorable news coverage and 'mentions' for their clients, both online and in the traditional media. PR is all about proper story positioning (the often maligned 'spin'), effective distribution and good media relations that all work together to improve an item's pick-up rate and usage. An effective PR effort gets people talking and creates positive 'buzz' through widespread (or even just well-placed) coverage, healthy pass-along readership and syndication, word of mouth and, in today's online world, online information sharing. The concept of social networking is based on sharing. Today's social networks, and their ability to spread a story very quickly, can be both a dream come true or a nightmare for a brand that is suddenly thrust into the spotlight. What's the old saying? Good news travels fast but bad news travels even faster? Negative information and malicious rumors can spread like a global wildfire online (and combining social networking with mobile email usage has sped up the process exponentially), *before* it gets picked up by the print and broadcast media. You must monitor your brand on an ongoing basis, including proper names, brand names and trademarks, to keep an eye on what people are saying about them online. 'Monitoring the conversation' has never been more important and an entire new industry, reputation management, has sprung up to provide that service for companies and executives that are concerned about maintaining the integrity of their brands online.

Communication tactics that build awareness and fall under the heading of potential PR tools include press releases aimed at the online, print and broadcast media, blogging and other forms of social networking, printed and electronic newsletters, public speaking opportunities and participation and sponsorship of local events. When you write and publish articles or are interviewed on topics that are relevant and interesting to your target audience, you raise your profile and reinforce your brand. When you link yourself to up and coming trends, emerging issues and other 'hot topics', you cultivate an image for yourself as a 'go to' and 'must know' person. All of these efforts will strengthen your light and actively broadcast it into the marketplace. This increases your visibility and makes it easier for the prospects and individuals whom you want and need to reach to hear about you, take action to learn more about you and, ultimately, find you.

Networking is an art and it is a very effective way to share your light with the world. In order to place your light into the path of people who can help you, you must be present (either in person or in spirit, through sponsorships and similar strategies) where members of your target audience can be found. In-person networking will always yield better results when you are first beginning to build a brand. Attend events produced and hosted by chambers of commerce, associations and local businesses, conferences and workshops, charitable events and gatherings that are specifically designed to bring networking businesses together (with each other and with potential customers). As with any strategy, focus your efforts on your target group, but be open and approachable by anyone. Often the most unlikely people can help you be successful, through their referrals and recommendations, by sharing expertise that you may not have known they possess, or by providing you with access to a resource that you may need. Be open to new networking opportunities, keep your expectations very simple and explore what the marketplace has to offer. Approach every networking opportunity as exactly that: an opportunity to connect with someone new. You never know where that connection will lead.

Partnering with other businesses to jointly reach out to customers through cross-marketing and other synergistic opportunities will increase the depth and breadth of your reach (and help you get greater mileage out of limited resources). Consider packaging services or products with complementary companies or participating in jointly-sponsored events that leverage your combined resources to attract something that all of the participants need to succeed (whether it be customers, investors or job applicants). Early in my career as an entrepreneur, I had an opportunity to help create and lead a business networking expo that attracted over 200 participants and brought business to business buyers and sellers together in one place, for four hours. It was very successful and I benefited not only by participating in the event, but also by reaching out to all of the other companies who sponsored or otherwise participated in the project. I gained a great deal of visibility by association, while also creating a business resource that benefitted many. It was a win-win, all the way around.

Never underestimate the importance of personal selling — of going out there, 'knocking on doors' (figuratively, not literally), introducing yourself and asking for the sale. You rarely get anything that you do not ask for (at least anything of value). I firmly believe that. Tell people what you would like them to do and what you are willing to do or offer in return. You will be surprised at how many people will respond positively to a clear, straightforward request that is posed in a forthright manner.

The Power of an Online Marketplace

The emergence of the Internet has changed the way that the world gets its information and the way that every company — and customer — does business. Individuals use the Internet to get news, to do research, to learn, to buy and to share information. Businesses use the Internet in much the same way. A business to business survey found that 85% of business buyers go online at some point during the buying process; that 83% of those business eventually bought from a vendor that they found online; and that 70% of the buyers had used a search engine to begin their search. Those percentages are no doubt increasing with each passing month. Online business to business buying and selling continues to evolve as market potential continues to expand.

The ways in which people make purchases has also changed dramatically. We have unprecedented access to product, price and service information. We can research products, compare products and read the comments of others who have bought the product before us. Our media habits have also changed dramatically, including where we get our news and how we learn about new developments and trends around the world. What we perceive as being 'important' is now influenced by many more factors than the daily newspaper or evening news of years past. The Internet has the power to spread stories (and scandals) in minutes, create 'overnight sensations' and make household names out of people and places whom we had never heard of before, almost instantly. Social networks are buzzing with information, true and otherwise. Managing that buzz has never been harder or more important.

The Internet has evolved from an entity that was originally used primarily for browsing, to a method to search and 'surf' and, today, as a tool to share, buy, learn, love and more. Anyone can post or share information, become a worldwide brand (in this world or a virtual 'second' one), a successful entrepreneur or an information creator, reseller and packager.

The Internet has leveled the playing field for businesses of every size and stage of development. It has never been easier or more affordable to become a 'global company', even if in image only. The Internet makes it possible for a company to market all of its products all of the time, and to reach out to highly targeted prospects in a very cost efficient manner. It is possible to create a successful business with very minimal resources. And: the Internet actually favors small businesses, which tend to move faster, be more adaptive and flexible, and have owners who are closer to the technology of their companies. These decision makers can spot, process and act on trends and marketing opportunities faster than their counterparts at larger companies and they typically have far less corporate or bureaucratic red tape to work through.

Much has been written about how the Internet provides any business with the capability to reach a global audience, but online markets have also become increasingly local in recent years. It has never been easier to find a business in your own neighborhood, just by searching by type and zip code. Consumers are discovering nearby companies that they never knew existed because they didn't drive by them on a regular basis or see their advertising. Small business owners can utilize online marketing strategies and advertising (in directories, guides, online mapping services and more, including GPS) to make it easy for local prospects find their stores and restaurants. They key, as always, is to Be Visible in order to Get Found.

A strong online brand will help you do that. Whether you are marketing yourself, your company or a product, how your brand comes across online will be critical to the success of your efforts. Many more people will 'meet you' for the first time online than in person, or even by phone or email. Your online image — and impression – must be a good one. Don't let random chance define your brand. Actively develop, manage, project and monitor your branding message to ensure that it is a true reflection of your light.

That's an important point to keep in mind. The Internet also gives you the ability to project your light much further. You can reach further and send yourself to places where you physically cannot be, through social networks, electronic marketing, video and real-time conferencing, low or no-cost global Internet long distance, text, IM and other forms of modern communication. You can *Be the Bulb!* and put your light in the path of prospects on the other side of town, across the country or around the world, with a similar amount of effort and investment. You can reach out and speak to people and prospects in a way that is highly relevant and personal (even intimate), and which can create relationships that are very strong by the time that you meet them in person or speak to them by phone should that ever happen. In today's online marketplace, most relationships never reach that level.

These people could be located half-way around the world or just across town and, regardless, they have equal access to information on your company. They may be shopping your store while you're asleep and while also checking out a competitor across the country or on the other side of the globe. They could know as much about your competition as you do and, at some point, are likely to talk to your current and former customers to hear what they have to say about your company. They will browse, learn, compare, make decisions and create a 'short list' of buying alternatives, often without any human interaction. You are unlikely to have an opportunity to sell them or state your case in person, by phone or even by email.

These invisible prospects have never been to your store or place or business, shaken your hand at a networking event or possibly even heard of you until just a few hours ago. Yet they've uncovered pretty much everything there is to know about your business by doing some searching online. And not only will they learn and make decisions on their own, they are also likely to share what they find (and decide) with members of their social networks.

You will be judged entirely by the quality of the image and information that you (or others) have put online, by how easy it is to access, and by whether its message appeals to their specific needs and interests. It has never been more important to make a good first impression because, quite frankly, one shot may be all that you get. Do not leave that impression to random chance. Take charge of your online brand and the message that it sends. Make sure that it is strong, clear, concise and on target. Think like a customer and act like a communicator. Be Visible, Get Found and RELATE to your target audience, in person and online. You know who they are. Make sure that they know who YOU are, and that they like what they find when they come looking for you.

Relationship building is very important in an online world, where most of the cues that you would normally use to communicate in a face-to-face situation with another person are absent. Your perceived image is the sum total of how you (and your brands) come across on your website and in your advertising, through your Google results and as a result of the buzz on the social networks. People who are meeting you for the first time online cannot see your store or your office, or the building and neighborhood where either is located. They have no idea what you are wearing or how well you dress on a daily basis. They can't see how you stand, shake hands or otherwise present yourself in person. You lose most of the cues that you provide (and vice versa) when you meet someone in person. Trust is very important to online relationship development. It is very important to convey confidence and create a sense of security for visitors who find you online so that they feel comfortable doing business with you, sight unseen. Remember how long it took to convince some people that it is safe to shop online? Remember how unusual it used to be for someone to use an online dating service or to do their banking online? All of these are commonplace practices today, but it took a lot of trust building to make people comfortable with replacing what were traditionally face-to-face transactions with online technology.

In branding, trust is everything. As consumers, we are willing to seek out and pay more for a brand because we believe we know what we will receive in return (the promise) and we feel that the promised result is worth the extra effort or money (reason why). Remember, a brand is a set of perceptions and experiences that we bring to a product or company. If we are in the brand's target market, those perceptions have meaning and value to us. We seek the brand out and we trust that it will deliver, as promised. That's why consistency in branding is so important, and not just in logo and image use, but also in how a brand's promise is conveyed. A brand becomes familiar when it, and its message, are presently strongly and consistently, and it becomes stronger when it delivers the experience that is promised, over and over again. Consistency creates trust.

We are about to move on to brand and message development. When you reach out to communicate with a global audience, words, images, phrases and even colors and body language can have different meanings in different countries, cultures and religions. You are about to enter a highly multi-cultural marketplace. Be mindful of what you are putting out there, especially if you are targeting a specific ethnic or cultural market. If you are not a member of that market, find someone who is and make sure that what you *think you are* saying is the message that is actually coming across.

Be The Bulb!

Chapter 9
Bright Shining Brand, Step by Step
(A Unique Brand Strategy)

Brand development is one thing. Brand communication, and consistency, is quite another. The message that you put out into the marketplace should truly reflect your brand and its offer, which should be relevant and meaningful to your target audience. Your message must be strong, clear, concise and on target. Think like a customer and act like a communicator. If you are not comfortable doing this, hire these services out. An entire industry has been built on the backs of people who have a talent for understanding what people want and need, and who know how to say, show and sell in a convincing way. Use their talents to create the strongest message possible.

The *Be the Bulb!* multi-step process is very much like a message development strategy. Both processes focus on developing, projecting and communicating energy at a target as a means of attracting attention and achieving a goal. As I've said, *Being the Bulb!* is very much about Being the Brand. Let's go back to our original diagram (next page) for the purposes of this section on brand development.

Both processes begin with identifying Core Strengths as a means of creating a Source of Motivational Energy. Core Strengths are the drivers behind our talents, our interests and our passions. They are born in us and inherent to who we are. Motivational Energy is created by identifying, cultivating and projecting the power that is generated by that Source. Products and brands are created, not born (although the process can be equally painful sometimes!). They are intentionally developed to possess a certain set of features and attributes which fill or solve a specific need, desire or role. They are created for a reason (or at least they should be). Whether that reason is a profitable one or not remains to be seen, but there is a

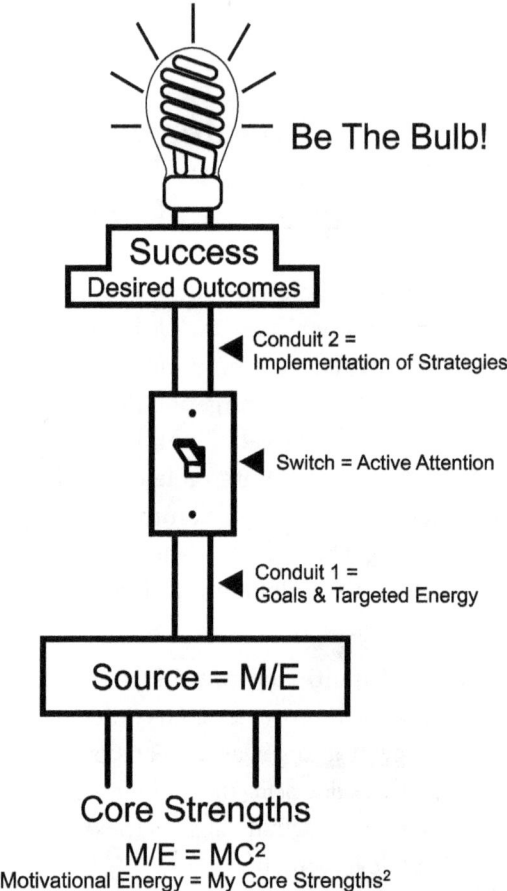

$M/E = MC^2$
Motivational Energy = My Core Strengths^2

reason — and at least the rudiments of a primitive selling strategy — at the birth of any product or brand.

For the sake of the following, we're going to focus on message development for a personal brand, although everything that you read will also apply to product or company branding. These are basic brand and message development lessons that you can use in many marketing scenarios. Learn them and you will become a much stronger communicator.

Step One of the branding process is all about identifying your Core Strengths and 'consumer' benefits. It is similar to the situation analysis in a business plan, where you analyze the marketplace that you are about to jump into. Know your market, know your competitors and, most importantly, know your product (yourself) and what it has to offer. This is where you identify your Core Strengths and create a context for them that will outline a path of opportunity to project your energy outward. You must understand the marketplace that you are entering in order to create Goals and Intentions that are meaningful to those who live, work and buy in that market. You have to be on an intimate basis with the needs and the opportunities of your target market if you want to be able to capitalize on your Core Strengths in a most productive way. Your Motivational Energy will feed on the dynamics of the marketplace and grow if you are tuned into its frequency and if you place your Motivational Energy, and your desire to succeed, in its context.

The next step is to Amplify your Core Strengths. Attraction Marketing is a method for creating and promoting your brand in a way which projects your energy into the marketplace and places it in the path of the people who can help you become successful. Amplifying your Core Strengths is a synonym for brand development. The basics of branding strategy all apply here. Focus on Benefits, not Attributes, and use them to develop a compelling promise with a strong Reason Why that is meaningful to your target audience. Be clear, consistent and do not over-promise. Brands grow stronger when they consistently deliver as promised. Consistency in service and quality are very important to building brand equity. You cannot say one thing and do another, unless you want to build a very different kind of reputation. What you say matters. What you do matters even more. Always deliver as you say you will.

No part of the process is more important than target audience development. You cannot set goals and intentions or lay the Conduit of the next step toward *Being the Bulb!* until you know who you want to reach out to and communicate with. Targeted Motivational Energy is very powerful. It is interesting, attention getting and very bright. Motivational Energy that is blasted out into the marketplace without direction or focus is not. Its power is diluted by being spread too thin. It becomes a glow at best, rarely worth more than a moment's notice. Your success — and the success of your business — will depend on your ability to identify and find the right people and prospects to speak to and to then speak to them (and with them) with words and in a context that they can understand and relate to. Choose targets whose needs, interests and desires match (or complement) your offering and you will greatly improve your chances for sales success. Remember, it is far better to reach 500 people who care about what you have to say than five million who have no interest in you, your services or your message. Quality definitely supersedes quantity in marketing. Define who your Ideal Customer is and then seek them out specifically. That's why it's called target marketing.

Defining your Ideal Customer is an important part of setting meaningful Goals and Intentions (creating the first section of Conduit). Ask yourself these questions to begin the process: What type of person is most likely to benefit from your product or service offering and why? What BENEFIT will they gain or derive from doing business with you? How important is it to them? How hard are they searching to find this benefit or are they not yet aware of their need? Can they obtain this benefit or a similar one somewhere else? Are they aware of the choices they have to fulfill their need? What is important to them? What do they value and does it coincide with what you have to offer? The answers to these questions will give you a feel for the 'problem that marketing can solve'.

Who are these people, specifically? What industries do they work in or what types of companies do they own or do business with? Where do they work and live, what do they read or watch, and where can they be found online? Are they early adapters, followers or late bloomers? Where do they go to do business, network, socialize, blow off steam or look for new ideas? What are the best ways to reach them? How do they make their buying decisions? Are they active researchers or passive receivers of new information? Describe them demographically (age, gender, geography, income, et al). What resources do they have? What resources do they need to do business with you? Are they willing to pay for your product or services? Can they? And, importantly, will working with them help you reach your own goals and feel successful? Many of these questions should have been answered when you first started working to identify your Ideal Customer.

It bears repeating: An Ideal Customer is someone who has a need, interest or desire for a product or service like the one that you are offering, is motivated to fulfill their need and has the resources, and the inclination, to perceive the value of your offering and pay for it, promptly. Yes, it's a lot to ask for but no, it's not impossible to find. These people are out there and they are your prospects. If you think about them and if you answer the above questions, you will understand who they are and how to find them. You probably already know people who fit the profile.

You cannot create an effective message unless you know who your Ideal Customer is and what is important to them. The Core Strengths of your brand must match the Benefits that your Ideal Customers need or want. There has to be a match. You may have to bring the need to their attention, but there has to be at least an elemental match of need with offering to make that possible in the first place. (Everything we buy satisfies some need. It may not be an obvious need, but a need always exists — even if it is only the need to be able to show ourselves or others that we *can* buy whatever is being sold.) Do not develop a message strategy until you know who you will be communicating to and with. There will be nothing to be gained from it.

A brand promise is a motivator. It identifies a need or a desire and promises to fulfill it. Attraction Marketing is *marketing by motivation*. It creates strong, bright energy that comes from Identifying and Amplifying Core Strengths and projects it into the marketplace in a targeted way which has meaning to its intended audience. It focuses on benefits, because benefits motivate people to take action.

Attraction Marketing motivates others to become aware of and interested in you and your offering. It motivates them to want to do business with you. Why? Because it takes targeted Motivational Energy, a strong message and consistent action and places it in the path of people who have an interest in that energy. By identifying your Ideal Customer and greatly reducing the size of the potential audience, you have created a target that is much easier to reach out to and make contact with.

Creating Measurable Goals is the next step in the process, whether you are on your way to *Being the Bulb!* or crafting your branding and messaging strategy. Define what you want to achieve and what success will look like once you get there. Make it all measurable so that it is possible to track your progress and compare the effectiveness of your strategies. Establish benchmarks that define where you are today, and set measurable goals for where you want to be tomorrow, next year and three years down the line. When you attach numbers and dates to goals, they become action plans. Creating action plans moves you forward through the Conduit and prepares you to Flip the Switch and enter the marketplace. Action plans are the preparation that precedes the perspiration. Do not skip this phase. 'Winging it' is not a strategy (or certainly not a good one).

At this point, you have identified your service and product offering and its benefits. You have identified who your Ideal Customer is and what is important to him or to her. You have created a list of attributes that describe this target and have determined Key Facts about them. Use what you have learned to take the next steps, which are positioning and message development. Your brand and its message should communicate how you and your offering are capable of satisfying and fulfilling the target's need or desire in a way in which no other competitor can do as well as you (or your product) can, or with as much value. That bears repeating: *Your positioning statement* (value proposition, USP, whatever you prefer to call it) *should communicate how you and your offering will satisfy and fulfill the prospect's need in a way which no other competitor can do as well, or with as much value.* The components of that value, the Benefits, will be based on the Ideal Customer profile that you created. It could be something tangible, such as a meal that satisfies hunger, or something that satisfies a much more intangible need such as status, belonging, love or security.

Your brand promise states how your offering will satisfy your Ideal Customer's need or desire. It defines your brand and will become the basis of your branding strategy, including your identity, message and media strategies. *What you do is as important as what you say.* Your actions must support your brand promise. Do not promise what you cannot deliver, but deliver what you promise, always.

Develop a message that conveys all of the above. If you are not comfortable in the realm of the creative, do not have a way with words or a feel for design, or if you are having difficulty in describing your Ideal Customer, call in the experts. Marketing and messaging are disciplines where the quality of the result is directly related to the level of expertise, insight and talent that is involved. Neither is a do-it-yourself proposition unless you happen to be a marketing or messaging expert. Understand what needs to be done and how the process works, but then go out and find someone who can develop your vision into a strategy that effectively reaches out to your Ideal Customer and communicates with them, utilizing a strategy that inspires action and results.

Does personal branding and promotion really involve as much work as product marketing? Absolutely! First impressions *do* count and especially in today's online marketplace, where you may only get one fleeting chance to make a strong and positive first impression. Are you willing to leave that one, all-important opportunity to random chance or, potentially worse, place it in the hands of an amateur? Of course not.

You are now ready to take the next step and it's a big one: Flipping the Switch and projecting your Motivational Energy and your message into the marketplace. Applying Active Attention (Flipping the Switch) PUSHES your brand forward and into the path of your prospects to make them aware of you and your offering. You have stated your goals, laid your plans and devised your strategies. Now you are ready to implement them.

Step Four, Flipping the Switch, requires a conscious, courageous act as you step forward, roll up your sleeves and tell the marketplace 'Look at me!'. This is where all of the work that you have done to prepare will begin to pay off. As with the lamp in your living room, the act of Flipping the Switch turns on the power and the light. As you actively implement your strategies and work your plan, you will become brighter and more visible, and you will light up the area around you. Applying more energy and effort will increase your reach and your brightness. It is the equivalent of installing a higher wattage bulb in a lamp. Work equals wattage. Effort equals energy. The more actively you apply Active Attention to your strategy, the more forcefully your Motivational Energy will move through the conduit, towards your prospects and toward the realization of your goals.

Results also create momentum. As people begin to notice you, they will reach back or gravitate toward you. As your efforts begin to pay off, even minimally, you will start to get excited. It works! Your enthusiasm will fuel your efforts and encourage you to push harder. Your bulb will burn brighter and the brighter your bulb burns, the more attention (and interaction) you will attract. It becomes a self-feeding and self-fulfilling process once you begin projecting your true, authentic light out into the marketplace.

Implementing your strategies occurs in the second section of Conduit, where channeling occurs. You are Putting It Out There as part of your strategy to Be Visible and Get Found and you are starting to create momentum. During this fifth step, it is important to keep your energy focused on your goals, be consistent in communicating your brand and to stay on target. Every time you project, promote or protect your brand clearly and consistently, you will make it stronger. Every time you deliver on your brand, as promised, you will create brand equity. If you truly believe in your goals and have confidence in your strategies, investing Active Attention in them will move your energy forward. Ignoring them will not. The best laid plans and strategies are meaningless if they are not followed. Implement your plan. Evaluate your progress, be flexible and make adjustments to your strategies where necessary, but stay on track and remain focused on your goals. Give it time to work. Give your light time to reach your audience. Give their energy time to come back to you, so that interaction can begin. Actively working your plan 'calls people into the room', where they can see, and explore, your light. *If you do not put your strategy to work, it cannot work for you.* I can't put it any simpler than that. You must take action, by applying Active Attention, and then work to stay on target through channeling. (That's why wishing and wanting on their own will never be enough to make your dreams come true. You must apply Active Attention to your goals and invest focused effort toward realizing them.)

Be the Bulb! Shine brightly, project your light forward and actively invite others to bask in it. *Be the Bulb!* in everything that you do. Choose to attract the attention and success that you want to come your way by putting your brand in the path of the people who can help you succeed and drawing them toward you. Place and keep your brand front and center with your target audience. Invite them 'into the room' where they can get a closer look at what you can actually do and deliver. Say what you mean and do what you say and your light will shine brightly. It will grow even stronger as others are drawn to it. Cultivate brightness, always.

Help your Bulb shine brighter by actively giving it attention, and not just when you are looking to get started or when sales are slow. *Being the Bulb!* means being your best and brightest self *always*. Once the light is on, keep it on. Do not 'turn it on and off' or 'apply as needed'. *Be the Bulb!* consistently and you will positively impact every facet of your life. Your energy will be contagious and it will bring many good things your way, if you devote the Active Attention — the effort — that your light needs and deserves.

Help your Bulb shine brighter by 'keeping it real'. Evaluate your strategies and your efforts from time to time to make sure that they are consistent with your brand and that you were on target with your original assessment and strategies. Time is a great teacher and greater clarity may come as you move through, and learn from, the process. Make sure that your efforts are taking you in the direction that you want to move, *toward the realization of your goals*. Movement in itself is not enough. Progress (forward movement) must be your goal.

Help your light reach further by thinking beyond your immediate market and circle. We live in a time when technology can take us around the world and back in a nano second, where time of day and traditional store and office hours have become meaningless. We can sell our goods on a street market in another country as easily as we can sell them at the mall in town. We can serve clients in person or virtually and in multiple markets, all at the same time. We are connected to people 'in degrees' through networks and social marketing and regularly exchange information and introductions with strangers. It has never been easier to meet people or harder, all at the same time, as many of us spend hours in front of a computer screen and away from face to face interaction. Explore and learn about technology and then leverage it to extend your light.

Keep your Bulb burning brightly by regularly fueling it with ideas, as well as enthusiasm. Be on the lookout for new ways to extend your brand and its reach. A brightly burning Bulb is clean, fresh, fully-powered and more effective.

Protect your Bulb from inertia by regularly revisiting your goals, assessing your progress and applauding yourself for your achievements. You are the primary power source. Build yourself up. Remind yourself how bright, energetic and powerful you are, and brainstorm new ideas for actualizing your Motivational Energy. *Being the Bulb!* is an evolutionary process. You should embrace it for the rest of your life.

When you interact and do business with other positive people you will move forward. When you find yourself in the company of negative, unhappy people you will not. Choose to protect your light and move forward, always. I'm about to show you how.

Part IV: Building on Success: Creating Entrepreneurial Synergy

Chapter 10
Keep Your Bulb Shining Brightly and Strong

Building your Motivational Energy and your light requires time, effort and focus. Your light is an asset. You must nurture and protect it to keep it bright and strong. Good gatekeeping will help your light grow stronger by inviting those who can facilitate your success to come closer and by keeping those who would drain your energy at arm's length. Regular brand assessment and 'maintenance' will prevent inertia and keep your light relevant and strong in a changing marketplace. Just as the bulb in your favorite lamp needs to be changed from time to time, your Bulb must also be replenished and given a fresh shine. Your willingness to assess, adjust and grow as necessary will keep your Motivational Energy strong and your light evolving in a world where similarly evolving needs, technology and products create new opportunities and buying choices every day.

How do you make your Bulb last longer and keep it from burning out? Replacing your Bulb is not as easy as putting a new bulb in the socket. Regular light bulbs have various life-extending features built in. Long-life bulbs are designed to operate at a lower filament temperature, which effectively extends their life. They don't burn quite as brightly, but they do last longer. Lowering the voltage required by a bulb also reduces the filament temperature and extends its life. Though energy efficiency is greatly increased, so is the amount of light that is given off.

Light bulbs typically burn out during the surge that occurs when they are turned on. Reducing the intensity of that surge does little to extend the life of the bulb. A worn filament is a worn filament. When it's over, it's over.

It takes some effort to get your Bulb burning and to get it burning at its brightest. You must protect your light from potential dangers and 'dimmers' to ensure that your Bulb continues to shine brightly.

Gatekeeping occurs at several key stages. It first comes into play when you assess your Core Strengths and refine your Motivational Energy. You are acting as a gatekeeper when you decide what represents a true Core Strength and then choose how (and on which strengths) you will focus your energy. Gatekeeping plays a role again once you have identified your Core Strengths, developed your goals and are working to devise your strategies. Strategies are plans and processes that you create to move yourself (or your company) forward. They are the 'how' for each 'what' that you set out to achieve. In the Motivational Energy diagram, strategies are represented by the first piece of Conduit that is laid. They are the channeling force that pushes your energy forward, as you prepare to Flip the Switch and apply Active Attention to your goals.

Gatekeeping at this stage requires you to direct your attention and effort toward the people and activities that will help you get where you want to go. Focus is key. Focusing on people who can help you and opportunities and activities that will move you forward directs valuable energy and resources to where they can do the most good. Good gatekeeping at this developmental stage will help ensure that when you Flip the Switch, you start off headed in the right direction. Gatekeeping keeps your energy moving forward to where it needs to go and prevents it from being diverted — and potentially siphoned off — by negative people whom you might meet as you make progress toward your goals. Gatekeeping will also keep you on the right track as your Bulb begins to shine.

Watch Out For Energy Suckers

Good gatekeeping ensures that you don't venture far from the Source and that your Motivational Energy stays pure. If you are selective in what and who you accept and allow into your life, you will remain true to your light. This applies to customers as well as friends, acquaintances and even loved ones. Every person who would appear to be willing or able to help you is not necessarily someone whom you should allow into your business or personal life.

Gatekeeping becomes critical as you make progress toward your goals and your light begins to shine brightly. When you project light into the marketplace, it is there for all to see. You can (and should) target and direct it at a specific audience, but you generally cannot keep others from feeling your energy or seeing your light. A strong entrepreneurial brand is magnetic and positive energy is contagious and attractive. This is the core tenet of Attraction Marketing. Your energy will attract others to its light and power. Many of these people will be similarly positive, energetic individuals who can help you grow or make progress toward your goals. These are the people who can help you get what you want or need, buy your products or services or put you in touch with other folks who will. They will applaud your efforts and toast your success, and they will encourage you and help you move forward. I like to think of these people as 'treasure hunters'. They know the power of positive energy and are drawn to it, whether they realize it or not. 'Like seeks like' and their positive energy will be drawn to yours. When you come together with them, for any reason, it can be very powerful.

Not all of the people whom you attract will have good intentions. Some will want to help you, buy from you or work with you. Others will just want to be with you or near you, to bask in and draw from your energy. Some will be downright draining. People like this have little light of their own and they do not know how to *Be the Bulb!* It is an entirely foreign concept to them that is beyond their comprehension. They don't know how to create Motivational Energy or channel it in a positive direction. Their energy goes into being negative or pessimistic and complaining about why things 'never go their way'. Their glass is always half-empty and falling — and that's on a good day.

Then there are individuals who are 'energy suckers'. Energy suckers are negative people who live in an absence of light. They are unhappy with themselves and the world around them and they focus what energy they have on complaining about what they don't like or don't have. They focus on what is lacking instead of what is possible, and they never tire of talking about it. They are more than pessimists, they are parasites — *and you cannot allow them to get too close to you*. They will drain your energy and dim your light, if you allow them to stay near.

You may find yourself wanting to help them — to listen to them, advise them and explain to them how they can build their own light. They have no interest in doing anything to improve their outlook. They are victims, not victors, and they exist on negative energy: their own and whatever they can create in the environment around them. Do not be drawn into the circle of their negativity or allow it to encircle you. These people will work very hard to get and stay close to your energy if they sense that you will allow them to. It is a parasite and a host relationship, and you will play the host to their dysfunctional need if you are not careful.

No doubt you've met someone like this before. We all know people who are never happy and leave us feeling drained. You can be on top of the world and they'll do their best try to knock you off, often very subtly. (It can be so subtle that don't realize what is happening or why you feel so tired after spending time with them.) They will use a variety of strategies to draw you in: pity, guilt and even anger, and they will turn on you if you do not 'feed' them with your attention. Be careful. Not every energy sucker is a sociopath, but some are. Don't let them get too close. You do not have to listen. You do not have to help. You do not have to be drawn into their world or their negativity. You have the ability to choose who you share your energy with. Choose to focus on being with and around positive people who can (and want to) help you build your light.

Be selective, not selected. Choose to *Be the Bulb!* and choose to keep your light shining bright by practicing good gatekeeping, always.

Protect Your Brand Assets

A carefully cultivated, successful brand is a valuable asset that must be actively protected. The more visible and successful a brand is, the more vulnerable it is likely to be. The time to take proactive steps to protect your brand is *before* it becomes a household (chat room?) name that is ripe for piracy or attack — not when the brand is already in crisis.

A SWOT (strengths, weaknesses, opportunities and threats) analysis serves as a good vulnerability analysis, as it considers hazards as well as benefits. A well thought out SWOT can raise the flag on potential points of weakness and danger in your brand. It can also identify opportunities to make it stronger. Here's another reason to undertake those regular brand assessments that I recommended earlier: They are especially helpful in developing and implementing a risk management plan for your brand.

Threats in the marketplace include piracy, brand confusion, brand attacks and cultural transcription or translation issues. Piracy is outright theft. Someone else knowingly uses or leverages the strength of your brand to lead customers their way instead of yours. Piracy can also result in brand confusion, where one company's product name, look, brand or marketing strategy is so similar to another's that potential customers begin to confuse the two. This has become especially problematic online, where search engine results are critical to helping prospective customers find and learn about brand and product websites. Speculators and pirates search out and claim intentionally deceptive brand-related domain names in an effort to confuse customers and exploit strong brands for their own benefit. It is nothing less than fraud, and every time a new domain extension is introduced (e.g. .mobi, .me), the potential for new piracy is born.

A brand attack occurs when an individual, a group or another company work to cause damage to your brand. They could be competitors, dissatisfied customers or total strangers but their goal is the same: to damage or destroy your brand by spreading negative information, rumors and other information on the Internet and among peer networks.

An unflattering or insulting translation (verbal) or transcription (written) of your brand and its slogan in another language can hurt a brand's global potential. Religious and cultural differences should also be considered before a brand is finalized. Be proactive and minimize these potential dangers by doing your homework during the brand development phase. If an unconsidered issue does raise its ugly head regarding your established brand, take action to correct the problem immediately, even if it requires a change in name or image. The positive publicity of doing the 'right thing' quickly and without question will help compensate for the costs of rebuilding the brand.

Online reputation monitoring and management is very important in today's marketplace and, like search engine optimization, it has launched an industry of its own. There are a number of cost and time-effective strategies that you can implement to manage your brand's 'buzz'. Create free Google alerts (or Yahoo or whatever your favorite search engine may be) to be among the first to know when the search engine crawlers find new information about you or your brand online. (You can create Google alerts for multiple names, phrases or topics by visiting www.google.com/alerts). Twitter, and other microblogging tools, are making it possible for users to share information faster than ever before. You can also create Twitter alerts and 'follow' people, topics and keywords.

It is a good idea to Google yourself, your brand and any related names or trademarks regularly, to see what the search engines show. Use multiple search engines. You'll be surprised at how different the results can be. Find something unflattering or negative? Creating social networking profiles, blogging and adding new, original content to your website (or contributing it to online e-zines) are just a few of the ways that you can build up positive hits — and your reputation — on the first few pages of your search engine results. You can produce positive results quickly and regular effort will really go a long way toward protecting your brand.

Creating a positive first impression has never been more important. In today's online marketplace, our reputations and the reputations of our companies and their products are managed by search engine results and online buzz. How we 'rank', what our search results say and whether the buzz about our products is positive matters — and it matters *a lot*. Proactive brand managers (and protectors) monitor what search engines and people are saying about their brands online and practice defensive visibility and ranking strategies that help control the results when potential customers, employers, mentors and the media search for information about their companies and their brands. When they find negative information or links, they respond decisively to move those negative search results down the list and out of the view of most search engine users.

How many times have you returned from a meeting (or a date) and immediately went to your computer to Google someone? When a brand becomes a verb, you know that it has entered the mainstream. Whether you use one of the major search engines or one of the thousands of smaller specialty sites, you are developing your initial 'brand' perception online whenever you search for information on a person, a company or a product.

Keep Your Bulb Shining Brightly and Strong

Today's search engines are reputation managers. You *are* your Google results to the people who do not personally know you, regardless of what the reality may be. First impressions really do count and if your first one isn't a good one, it's likely to be your last. Do not leave your search engine results — and what they say about you — to chance.

One strategy for protecting your brand online and for influencing the first few pages of its search engine results is to have one or more websites with domain names that feature your name, your company's name and the names of its major brands. Purchasing domain names is not enough. Only live websites that have content are ranked by the search engine crawlers. They can be very simple, but they have to be active. Parking a static page won't have a big impact on your results. Publishing a blog is another good online reputation management strategy. Use free blog publishing and hosting services such as Wordpress.com and Blogger.com and include your name or your brand name, your blog's domain name or your primary key word in your blog's domain URL. Then publish at least weekly. Search engines love original content that is freshened regularly. Often, when I add a new post to my blog, the Google alert comes through as quickly as the next day.

Creating profiles on social networking and business networking sites will allow you to claim your name and brand and build your online reputation. Skip the nicknames and use your real name and brand names to maximize your search engine rankings. Myspace.com and FaceBook.com are popular social networking gateways. Linkedin.com can be a great tool for promoting yourself and for making new business contacts. Some sites even make it possible for you to create your own social networking community. Check out Ning.com and consider the possibilities for creating a network that is focused on you and your brand, or an issue that is important to your business or product category.

Your first step should be to lay claim to your name online before someone else does. Create profiles and enable them for public view (so the crawlers and others can find them). Websites like Naymz.com allow you to create a profile and link all of your other profiles to it. It also creates another (often-cited) search engine reference. Your goal should be to create as many positive references and links as possible so that the first few pages of your Google or other search engine results page are dominated by 'happy news' about you and your brand. Search engine optimization will also help improve your rankings. Have an expert help you with meta-tags and keywords on your website to improve the chances that it will be found. Submitting your website to the search engines, both large and small, will also help. Anything that you do to improve your online presence — to Be Visible so that you can Get Found — will also help generate positive search results. It is a win-win when you invest time in building your online presence and profiles. Skip one of your favorite television shows and invest at least an hour or two a week in refining and expanding your reputation monitoring and managing strategies. You will see measurable results quickly.

Other online brand and reputation management strategies include posting comments on other people's blogs (with a link to your website embedded in your posting signature), sharing photos on sites such as Flickr.com, creating a Wikipedia entry (harder) or a wiki (easier) using free online wiki creation resources (Google it!). Link your website with popular, trusted websites whenever possible. (Inbound links from government or educational sites that end in .gov or .edu are especially good for SEO.) Use 'pay per click' advertising on the major search engines (Google, Yahoo, MSN) to ensure that your brand appears on the right hand (paid side) of the results. People who pay attention to that side of the results page are typically motivated buyers.

Keeping an eye on your brand's online reputation can be relatively hands-free if you do some set-up work on the front end. Create a Google alert for your name, your brand, any brand slogans or trademarks, key people in your organization and anything (or anyone) else that you want to monitor. It's free. There are also a number of websites that will help you search and track social networking commentaries and mentions. The list of available sites and tools changes almost daily, it seems. Search for 'track buzz on social networks' or 'reputation management' on your favorite search engine to review the most current offering.

Watch the blogs carefully. They can be as harmful as they are potentially helpful to your brand. In today's marketplace, prospects are more

Keep Your Bulb Shining Brightly and Strong

likely to hear, read or learn something online as they are from a national newscast or the print media. And they will hear it, read it and learn it *faster*. Watch the major blog sites such as Technorati, Bloglines, and Twitter (microblogging) and the Blogger and Wordpress top feeds to track your online mentions and buzz so that you can be among the first to know when you or your brand is being talked (or twittered) about.

If you find something negative, you must take action. It is difficult to remove a link to a negative comment, blog post or website completely, but you can take steps to push the undesirable result back to a later page (where most people seldom venture). Use strategies like those that follow to rebuild your online reputation if you become the subject (or the target) of a negative news story or brand attack.

If you don't have a website, create one immediately and load it with original, positive content. Buy additional sub-domains that include you or your brand's exact name, slogan or a relevant phrase and set up mini websites that have original content. Search engines consider these as separate hits. They won't count for much in the beginning, but every little bit helps. Your goal should be to create unique, positive mentions that are keyword linked to your brand. Lots of them.

Start a blog, or a second blog and focus on good news about yourself, your company or your brand and your industry. Post regularly and keep it positive, but not too overly self-serving (you still need to make a good first impression with people who find it). Build your brand while you are rebuilding your reputation. Stay on message and on target. Comment on and link to other blogs mercilessly (with thoughtful, interesting comments that get picked up and shared by others). Expand your social networking net and create profiles on every possible site. Freshen your existing profiles and add photos or links to them. Join an online community or two and buy an online ad or link. Post groups of photos, logos or other artwork (with your name or brand attached to them) separately on Flickr.com. Each group will count as a separate hit.

In short, if you want to push down negative search results, implement, accelerate and build on the online branding strategies that you should be using anyway. Actively promote your brand online and you will be well ahead of the game if you ever have to respond defensively.

It is nearly impossible these days to 'manage the online conversation', which is going to take place with or without you. Search, monitor, listen and participate when appropriate (meaning that you have something of value to add). You can initiate a topic (on your own blog, a discussion board or elsewhere) and see how it develops, but you will not be able to control it (influence, yes; control, no). Author, blogger and marketing guru Seth Godin summed it up this way on one of his insightful blog posts at Sethsblog.com: "It's a brand cocktail party! You get to set the table and invite the first batch of guests, but after that the conversation is going to happen with or without you."

Make sure that you're at the party to hear what's being said about you and your brand (and your competitors). Monitor your online reputation and manage it proactively and your Bulb will continue to burn brightly.

Chapter 11
Be A Good Gatekeeper

Learning to be a good gatekeeper is important to keeping your energy positive and your Bulb shining brightly. Some of the greatest threats to your Motivational Energy and will be presented by people who come into your life, either directly or peripherally.

Intention is a powerful thing. We all send signals that attract certain types of people into our business or personal lives. Your brightly shining Bulb will attract a lot of people to you. Not all of them will be positive, even though they will be drawn to your positive energy.

How do you attract these people in the first place? Often, it is because you didn't target sharply enough and cast too broad a net with your energy. Like moths to a flame (or a backyard porch light), negative people will be drawn to your light along with the positive, productive people that you are actively working to attract. Positive, energetic individuals who have a passion for what they do create a magnetic aura that pulls people toward them. You are learning how to become one of those people. Part of the process must include learning how to avoid being overwhelmed by attention, and particularly negative attention.

If you project your energy outward in a non-specific effort to attract people of *any* kind – whether as customers, partners, vendors or whatever — that is exactly what you will get: any, *and every*, kind of people.

Know your target audience and be specific with your intentions. Know the types of people whom you want to attract and direct your energy at those targets. When I first moved to Arizona, I was looking to meet other women and make some new friends. I targeted my efforts at meeting women in a certain age group, instead of searching for women who had similar energy, attitudes and interests. My first few 'relationships' went badly. The women were needy and unhappy and generally very draining to be around.

Our time together was often spent with me listening to them complain about what they didn't have or couldn't live with or without. There was a lot of drama, much of it repetitive, and I would always feel tired and 'down' after spending time with them. These women were literally draining the energy out of me. Once I realized what was happening, I made a conscious effort to sit down and think about (and write down) the types of female friends that I really wanted to attract into my circle. The results were dramatically different and almost instantaneous. Within a few weeks of clarifying my intention, I ended up meeting and making a number of very good woman friends, including one who became a business partner in another venture.

This has also happened to me in my professional life. We all have times when we are looking to attract new business, and sometimes we feel as if might take any kind of work just to keep the money coming in. Whenever I have adopted that attitude — that *any* customer is a good customer if they have money — it has always (without exception) worked to my disadvantage and I have lived to regret it. I ended up with clients who were difficult to work with, misrepresented the scope of the project or the work that needed to be done, or didn't pay on time — not a productive or profitable scenario by any means. When I consciously look for clients who fit the profile of the types of people and companies that I want to work with, things always turn out much better. Our respective energies and passions are a match from the start and our relationship usually continues productively, for both of us, for many years. The better I focus and choose, the more mutually beneficial — and profitable — the relationship proves to be. There have been very few exceptions to this rule.

Here is a motto that I work very hard to live by: 'Be Selective, Not Selected'. (Or: Be the chooser, not the chosen.) The power to create your own reality, and to keep it positive and productive, lies in keeping the power of choice in your hands. You have chosen to *Be the Bulb!* and to let your light shine through. You have chosen how you will target your energy and how you will direct your light. Now you must choose who you will allow to draw near and stay. Making this choice with care, strength and purpose will help your light shine even brighter. And yes, you can apply this principal in both your personal and your professional lives.

You can influence the types of people that you attract by targeting your Motivational Energy. (You cannot control it completely, but you can influence it.) Gatekeeping adds an additional filter that helps ensure that your efforts stay on track and that your Motivational Energy remains strong. It ensures that the negative people who come into your life do not get close enough or stay long enough to drain valuable energy from you. In my workshops, I talk about strategies for protecting a brand, online and off. Gatekeeping helps protect the positive energy that you, your company and its brands project into the marketplace. It helps keep that energy pure and strong so that your Bulb continues to shine brightly.

Some of the people you encounter will be just plain negative. They suffer through life and can suck the air — and the light — out of a room in a heartbeat. These people can turn a good day into a bad one almost instantly — *but only if you let them.* You know who they are. You have felt them in your life. You have worked with them, for them and against them. If they are still in your life, let them go. Do not try to help or 'fix' these people. They do not want your help. They only want your energy. Focus your energies on people who can help you succeed, whether in business, in relationships or in life. Match your positive energy with the positive energy of others and you will create greatness. Entrepreneurs are builders and creators by nature. Target customers, employees, partners, suppliers and investors who are willing — and motivated — to grow and succeed with you.

Sometimes the negative people you attract will be a reflection of your own insecurities or uncertainties. You subconsciously attract them because they are like your weaker self. You can prevent this from happening by making sure that you are truly focused on your Core Strengths. Focus on your strengths and not on your weaknesses and you will attract what you want and need in your life. This applies to both product and personal brands. You will get back what you put out into the marketplace in terms of energy, motivation and message. If your brand is truly strength based and your branding strategy and promise reflect that truth, you will attract people and customers who feel a connection — and a need — for your offer.

When you change the way that you look at the world, your world will be forced to adapt and change its reaction to you. Sir Isaac Newton was right. Every action does have an equal and opposite reaction. If something moves forward, something must move back in response. The greater the push forward, the greater the push back must be. A change in direction requires a relative change in reaction. Likewise, a change in attitude will typically bring a change in reaction, especially by the people who are closest to you.

Evolution creates change and change is stressful. There may be people who have been in your life for a while who do not like the new brighter, shinier, more positive you. People generally like knowing what to expect from life and they find comfort in maintaining the status quo in their relationships with people and products. The relationship that an individual develops with a brand can be, by nature, very personal. If the brand changes or evolves too dramatically, the foundation of that relationship will also change. The result? You should expect to see some attrition in your business and professional lives as you begin to truly focus on strength-based branding and marketing. Some customers will move on, but others will arrive to take their place. It may become stressful as things ebb and flow, but it will be productive, growth-oriented stress. The long-term results will be more in keeping with your goals and you will find yourself much more capable of enjoying real success when it does come your way.

When you grow and evolve personally and professionally, there are always going to be people who will be more comfortable with the way that you 'used to be'. They may actively work to block your evolution or even try to change you — or your brand — back toward the person or product that they were comfortable with. (Remember Newton and the 'push back' principle.) Do not let them redirect your Motivational Energy or dim your light. Continue moving forward. As you get in touch with your Core Strengths and begin to build a brand that is better focused on who you are, some of your past assumptions (and relationships) will be proven wrong and may no longer fit well with your new set of (truer) goals. Stay positive, stay focused and be true to the progress that you are making. The people who are close to you in your professional and personal lives will either evolve along with you (though on their own paths) or you will have to continue moving forward without them. And please note: Every word of this paragraph applies to the customers you serve through your business as well as the people whom you deal with in your personal life. Every customer relationship doesn't have to be forever, nor should it be. Evaluate your customer relationships on a regular basis to make sure that they fit the way that you want and need to do business. You may find that some of your customers actually have a negative impact on your business due to their excessive service or pricing demands, the logistics of serving them or even the attitude that they bring to the table. Choosing who you will do business with is an important part of *Being the Bulb!*

Gatekeeping is an art that requires good intuition and some flexibility. 'Guarding the gate' too well may cause you to miss some important opportunities. Do not dismiss people who do not fit your intentions or your Ideal Customer profile too quickly. They may represent a unique customer category or a new selling opportunity that you haven't considered. Do not equate different with negative. There is great value in having different types of people in your life whom you can learn from. Diversity is good, and not just for the obvious reasons. You will grow as an individual and as a business owner by being open to opportunity and by welcoming new ideas and influences into your world. You can usually learn something, good or bad, from everyone you meet. Don't create boundaries (gates) that keep learning opportunities away. Strive to continue learning and growing, without being drained of your energy by the negative people that you will likely meet. This is what makes good gatekeeping so challenging.

You can become an effective gatekeeper by following a few basic strategies. These guidelines will help strengthen your intuition and assessment skills.

Know who and what you are trying to attract and be very specific in your intention. Refer to the goals and intentions that you created to realize the full potential of your Core Strengths and keep your target customer profile top of mind. The conduit that you created exists for a reason. It is a framework to guide your energy in the most productive direction. When you stray from it, your energy will be diluted or misdirected. Most people enter our world for a reason, either to help us move forward in some way or to help us better clarify what we want and need. If people do not fit the profile that you have created, don't send them packing too quickly. Determine whether there is something productive that you can learn from them, or they from you. (It may not always be positive.) We grow by interacting with and helping others and the energy that your efforts create will move both parties forward. Be protective of your space, but not overly protective. Toxic people teach us what we don't want in our lives and the best lessons learned are often the difficult ones.

Setting personal boundaries is an important part of gatekeeping, especially in the workplace. Boundaries are essential for preserving energy, but they should not be barriers to productivity or create insurmountable walls with peers, associates, co-workers, customers or potential clients. Professional boundaries should be like stone markers along a path: they define the limits of the space and offer a sense of direction, but they do not block progress or prevent anyone from entering or exiting the relationship at any point. Think of boundaries as flexible relationship 'guidelines' that you can strengthen or take down at will. If your boundaries are too tall or too strong, they will block the flow of energy back and forth. If they are too weak, they will allow too much to clutter your path.

Be clear about who you are, what you want and what you have to offer. Ambiguity is an invitation for people to 'test the limits' of your boundaries. Be consistent in what you communicate, how you work and the quality of the service that you deliver. Strong brands are always clear and consistent. *Being the Bulb!* is also about Being the Brand. Make sure that people know what to expect from having a professional or personal relationship with you. Focus on your Core Strengths and base your boundaries on the values that are inherent to your goals and intentions. Strength of purpose and message create tangible, effective boundaries that make it easy for people to know how to interact with you or your company.

There's another factor that you should consider when it comes to personal branding and the impression that you are putting out into the marketplace. Whether you like it or not, you are known by the company that you keep, both personally and professionally. The group of people whom you choose to surround yourselves with sends a message to the marketplace. Your client and customer lists are a reflection on your business, as are the groups that you choose to associate yourself with at and outside of work. If you do business with Fortune 500 companies, you will attract other Fortune 500 companies. If you do business with struggling small businesses, although a very worthy pursuit, you are likely to attract other struggling small businesses. Every business is created for a reason. A key part of that 'reason for being' is usually to serve a specific group or type of customers. No matter how large or how small, every business must have a customer target and profile that is driving the way that they do business. When you try to be everything to everyone, no one receives the service or attention that they need and deserve.

It's also a fact of life that some customers are simply better to do business with than others. Know who your Ideal Customer is, what's important to them and why they are a good match for your company. This Ideal Customer may be a heavy user who values service and relationships over price, pays promptly and likes to refer new business your way. Customers like these are simply better to work with. Difficult customers are often less profitable and they can have a negative impact on your business in terms of efficiency and morale. They can also negatively impact your relationship with your 'good' customers by absorbing company resources through their excessive demands, service requirements or slow pay habits.

It's no secret that eighty percent of a company's business often comes from twenty percent of its customers. Strive to make that top twenty percent the very best twenty percent that it can be and you will end up improving the overall quality of your other customers. Like tends to attract like. Your customers want to work with a company that is familiar with their needs and the needs of their industry. Your customer list is your resume that says a lot about the markets you serve and the way that you do business.

Use the profile that you created for your Ideal Customer as your primary gatekeeping criteria. Be true to the profile and your intentions. Give it attention and weed out the 'wannabes' and the high maintenance customers who take away more than they give. Do it gracefully and without calling attention to your actions. You do not want to damage your company's reputation or brand, or start a backlash of negative buzz in the marketplace. Alter your messages and your marketing strategies to better attract the types of customers whom you really want to do business with. Your goal is to create boundaries without building walls. Know who you need and want to do business with and then go after them. Be focused, but also be flexible. You need to stay on target but also open to opportunity at all times. If you are truly tuned into the energy (and the cues) around you, your intuition will kick in and you will know when a little leeway could lead to a productive new path. There's really very little guesswork or risk involved. The brighter your bulb shines, the more information and opportunities you will attract. Successful entrepreneurs are always processing information. That's why they're usually ready to act quickly when opportunity comes their way. They are rarely getting started from scratch.

They've also gotten good at saying 'no'. Being able to let go of strategies that aren't working, relationships that aren't productive, information that isn't relevant or customers who may be less than ideal helps successful entrepreneurs maintain their focus. It can be very hard to say no to prospects or existing customers who are too hard to work with or do not have the potential to help us move forward, especially in a highly competitive marketplace or a less than stellar economy. If you are attracting a lot of customers who fit this profile — who are demanding, unhappy, hard to work with or satisfy, or who always bicker over their invoices — it is time to review your original target marketing strategy to ensure that 1) it accurately presents and amplifies your Core Strengths; 2) you are targeting your energies correctly; and 3) that you are executing your strategy correctly. Revisit the first and second stages of Conduit and review each step to determine where you may be misdirecting your energy. You may be focusing on Attributes instead of Benefits, or missing the Competitive Benefit and/or Reason Why that your true target is searching for. Make sure that the message that you are communicating is the one that your target prospects want — and need — to hear. It must be relevant and resonate with their needs in order to put you on their radar.

A word about diversity is appropriate here. Gatekeeping has nothing to do with types of people. It is about the *qualities* and *energy* that an individual (or a company) brings to the table as a potential customer in terms of opportunities for increased volume, margin and profitability for your business. Your Ideal Customer is a factor of the Benefits that your company's products and services offer. Strength-based branding appeals to prospective customers who have interests and needs that complement your offering. You may find that it is easier or more profitable to work with small companies versus large, established companies or startups, or to work with non-profits versus Fortune 500 companies. You may even choose to run a business that gives away its products or services on a pro bono basis and finds its funding sources elsewhere. It is your business and your choice — as long as your choices are not based on sex, race, religion or any other type of individual discrimination.

There will be times when you simply cannot avoid having negative people in your life, whether due to employment situations, family relationships or customer dynamics that you have no ability to change. These people are called energy suckers for a reason. They are the 'dimmer switches' that can potentially lower your energy and your light. You may have to deal with these people, but you don't have to let them 'in' or make it personal. Take the spotlight off of them by refusing to be drawn in by their negativity. Do not focus your energy on them or give them the attention that they want and need, despite their continuing efforts to impose themselves in your life. They are drawn to your light but they will only linger if you allow them to stay by enabling them. Recognize them for what they are and keep them at arm's length. Focus on your Motivational Energy and the positive people and opportunities that it attracts. The negative ones will eventually move on due to lack of attention.

Whom you choose to allow into your energy field is up to you and you alone. Be open to opportunity but make choices that are right for you. Look for people whose values reflect your values and whose energies complement yours in nature (positive) and strength. *When two sources of positive energy come together, the result is always very powerful.*

Chapter 12
Avoid Inertia and Burnout

Being the Bulb! is going to change your life. It is going to transform the way that you approach the world and the way that the world reacts to you. It is going to infuse new energy into everything that you do, including — and especially — your business. Everything that you do and touch is going to be brighter, better. People who meet you are going to want to be with you and work with you.

When things are going well, it's human nature to want to take your foot off the pedal and coast for a while. When you work hard, it's nice to be able to take time to bask in your own light and your own success.

A strong, established brand can coast on its own for a short time. Personal brands are much the same way. If you have built a strong reputation for living up to your brand, your brand can function on auto pilot for brief periods of time. You can take a break from promoting your brand, as long as you maintain product quality and service. Even the strongest brands will deteriorate quickly if they do not live up to their promise. It is all right to take a deep breath once in a while and sit back, but you must *Be the Bulb!* and 'be the brand' always. It can take years to build a strong, successful brand and only one minute — or a single incident — to destroy much of what you've worked for. It is the reality of the world that we live in that bad news travels much faster than good. Sadly, many people find it more interesting. People are also much more likely to tell others about a bad experience that they've had with a product or company than they are to relate a story about a good experience. Be on your best brand behavior always.

Taking time out to stop, look around and assess the marketplace is, however, important to your brand's survival. These moments of pause are good times to assess your brand and your light, and to ensure that they are an accurate reflection of who you are (your Core Strengths), what you want to have (your Intentions) and what you want to achieve (your Goals). Regular brand assessment is important to any communication or marketing effort and it is no different when you are *Being the Bulb!* Strong brands evolve with the marketplace to meet changing needs, competition and other factors. Your light must similarly evolve. A static brand is not a strong one. Inertia is your enemy and it can negatively impact your brand. Assessment and evolution will help keep it relevant, fresh and vital.

Newton's first law of motion defines inertia as 'the tendency of objects to remain in motion or to stay at rest unless acted upon by an outside force'. Some business owners continue moving ahead until something gets in their way and slows them down or stops them. They feel that 'all is well' unless they are faced with a speed bump or some kind of road block. You've heard the expression: 'Don't fix it if it ain't broke'. That's only partially true. A much better strategy to follow is to 'make sure that it isn't near the breaking point' or 'try to spot cracks before they become fissures'. We all know that preventive medicine and maintenance can help us avoid large medical and repair bills. It works the same with your light and your brand. If you pay attention, watch the marketplace, listen to your customers and keep an eye open for changing needs and competitive circumstances, you will ensure that your Motivational Energy and your light remain on track. Remember, your Conduit is directed at a target, a goal. That target can move whether you want it to, or will it to, or not. If you do not move with it and adjust your aim, you will not stay on track and you will not reach your goals. Your message may lose its relevance. Your product or service offering may become just a little bit 'off'. Talk about missing the target! Even the best laid plans, the strongest energy and the brightest light can fail to take you to your goal if you do not keep your eyes on the target — and especially as it moves.

Your entrepreneurial life, like life in general, must always be a *work in progress*. Your Core Strengths are inherent to who you are and do not change, but just about everything else around you will. Other people change, the marketplace changes, circumstances change, the world changes and your relationship with all of them will change and evolve. We must grow and evolve as humans. We must develop as business owners and entrepreneurs. Our lives continually change because of either and both, and the world will keep spinning and changing around us whether we like it or not. We have to be a work in progress.

Change is inevitable. Growth is your goal. You must avoid inertia by working to ensure that your offering and your message remain relevant. You must keep your sites focused on the target as it moves to ensure that you remain on track and moving toward your goals.

As entrepreneurs, we make careers out of making choices. We choose our paths to pursue our passions. We choose partners and employees, products and services to offer, business structures and sectors to serve, organizational plans and missions, marketing strategies and vehicles. We make choices that affect every part of our business life every day, beginning on the day that we choose to go into business for ourselves.

Choose to avoid inertia and become your own life's work.

There's an ancient Chinese proverb (are there any modern ones?) that says: "If we don't change where we are going, we'll probably end up there." Does the road that you're on right now lead to where you want to go? Maybe it has adjusted its course since you first stepped onto it. Or maybe you are the one who has changed course. Perhaps a better path has presented itself, or is about to open. Keep your eyes on the road — and the target — to watch for opportunities to grow, evolve or even change direction. Life is not static. Accept that truth, embrace it and work with it, not against it. It is the best way to keep your brand dynamic and strong.

Inertia is not inevitable. You can take steps to fight it. Never stop looking around or learning. Change is happening everywhere around you. Pay attention to it and learn from it, and use what you learn to adapt your business. Being an entrepreneur and a business owner is a never-ending, lifelong pursuit. There will always be opportunities to make your company stronger, smarter and more successful. Even if you do not want to make it 'big' (and many business owners don't), there is always room to make it stronger or more efficient. Look for these opportunities. They are out there in the universe and in the marketplace and new ones present themselves daily to those who are watching, listening and ready to take action.

Don't let your business plan get dusty. You put a lot of work into developing it in the first place. Read it. Use it. Review it regularly and use the benchmarks that it includes to evaluate your progress toward your goals. Is your ETA (estimated time of arrival) on track, or did you wander from your original route? Perhaps a new or faster route has presented itself since the time that you originally created your plan. Re-evaluate the marketplace around you and consider it in the context of the document that you hold in your hand. Regular assessments and some well-considered fine tuning is a sure cure for inertia — and the only real way to ensure that your business plan remains relevant to your company's (and the marketplace's) current situation.

Look at your business in the same way that your customers see it and evaluate it. Is your product and service offering relevant and competitive? Is your marketing message meaningful? Is your service as good as you want it to be? In these busy times, dissatisfied customers rarely take the time to complain. They just leave. It's easier. A lack of complaints or negative reviews (online or off) does not necessarily mean that everything is fine. Evaluate every part of your company's prospecting, selling, service and follow up process just as any customer might and identify strengths and weaknesses. A mini SWOT (strengths, weaknesses, opportunities and threats analysis) will provide you with a potential action plan and some good food for thought. Use it to make sure that your company isn't just 'going through the motions'. Strong brands and companies should be in a constant state of *considered evolution*. Evolution builds on strengths and works to eliminate weaknesses. When you choose to *Be the Bulb!* you are making a conscious choice to build on your strengths, project the positive Motivational Energy that is created and use it capitalize on opportunities in the world around you. Your energy and your brand should always be evolving to keep pace with the marketplace and its changing opportunities.

Evolving brands — and businesses — thrive. Static brands die. Change for the sake of change is not the prescription. *Considered brand evolution is.*

An evolving brand stays strong and on target. It keeps pace with the marketplace and with competitors. Most importantly, it stays relevant to changing market needs. Your Core Strengths can find an outlet in many different ways. The same is true of your business and your entrepreneurial spirit. An entrepreneur looks for opportunity in the marketplace and acts on it. Serial entrepreneurs repeat the process, over and over again. Entrepreneurship implies 'newness': new products, new services, new companies, new ways of doing things and new ways of looking at existing concepts. New doesn't have to be 'brand new' or completely unique. Newness can also come from making your offering discernibly different, more competitive, more intuitive, easier or more fun to use or simply better in some easily identifiable, quantifiable way. (As opposed to saying 'new and improved' just for the sake of it.) 'Sameness' is not a goal that successful entrepreneurs strive for. Better or, ideally, *best* certainly is.

Businesses that fail to evolve and adapt will be left behind by the marketplace and the customers who do business in it. This is especially true in today's markets, where change occurs more frequently, more rapidly and with far less fanfare. A strong, evolving brand stays on strategy, but evolves in ways that keep it fresh, meaningful and top of mind. That same brand, however, never strays too far from its Core Strengths or core message. This protects its Motivational Energy, or 'reason for being', from being compromised. If a brand's original purpose or use has changed drastically, more than an evolution may be called for. Major changes in customer needs or wants, the introduction of new technology and products, or the entry of a new competitor or a unique business model will require a brand re-assessment and a potential change in strategy. Stubborn brands that refuse to acknowledge the need for change will not succeed in the long run.

In some cases, the marketplace may prove a branding strategy to be misdirected, or founded on inaccurate information or poor assumptions. Make the time and invest the effort to review, repair or change the strategy, and drastically, if necessary. This is a brand correction, which requires swift, definitive action. Evolution is more of a gradual, sometimes barely discernible process. Think of evolution as a 'facelift' that freshens your brand as the years go by. The goal is not to scare off satisfied customers, but to assure their continued satisfaction and continue to add to their numbers as they, the marketplace and your brand evolve.

Don't over-react, but don't fail to react either. Strong brands, whether personal or product, are proactive. Their managers and mentors work to anticipate change and to lead it, gently, and in an evolutionary and logical way. A brand revolution is best left for new product introductions or complete re-branding efforts. Revolution usurps the status quo and requires re-introduction and education. Existing customers may find themselves suddenly dissatisfied with what has essentially become a new brand. Certainly they may become confused.

That's an important point to keep in mind. A brand is a perception that people have about you, your company or its products. It is based on experience, which includes the ways in which prospects have been exposed to your brand, their experience with it and the experience of others whom they interact with. *You cannot change experience, but you can reposition it.* You can reframe experience and perception in ways that can help these thoughts and feelings evolve with your brand by building on the foundation of strengths and preferences that the brand already has with its customers. Public relations professionals do this all the time by 'framing' or 'spinning' a story. How an offer is framed and presented has a huge impact on how it is perceived and received. Perception is not necessarily reality, but it is the number-one influence on buying behavior. Successful brand evolution requires you to encourage — and manage — a parallel evolution in customer perceptions. The entire brand experience has to evolve.

And as your brand promise evolves and changes, continue to make good on it, always. That rule never changes.

Tactics for encouraging successful brand evolution include regularly talking with or surveying customers to find out what's on their minds and how it relates to your brand. Stay current with what's relevant to your brand's existing proponents through focus groups, surveys and one-on-one phone calls. Then use what you learn and compare your brand to existing realities and perceptions to make sure that it is not just on track, but on the same track that your target customers are tuned into.

Put new technology to work to present your brand in new and interesting ways both online and off to keep it looking fresh and current. Having a website is not enough. Having a multi-tiered social networking and viral marketing strategy is a beginning. Creating an integrated marketing strategy that reflects the evolution in shopping and buying habits, and working it, continually, is essential. Stay up to date with how prospects are searching for, finding — and sharing — product information and look for ways to insert your brand into those environments. Remember: *Attraction Marketing puts your brand in the path of people who can help you succeed.* It is no different with product brands. A brand has to be seen, and noticed, in order to be part of the conversation, and it has to Be Visible in order to Get Found. Put your brand where its prospective customers are. Do not force them to go looking for it in unfamiliar places. They won't.

Introduce new ways to present your brand, such as innovative advertising strategies, leveraging new technologies or communicating with prospects in new (and meaningful) ways. Keep in mind that once 'everyone is doing it or using it', it is probably time to look for a new way to stand out. Sameness — in products or brands and their promotion — does not create top-of-mind awareness or standout competitors. If you choose to go with the crowd, you will likely get lost in the crowd. It's as simple as that.

Successful, evolving brands create and attract buzz, which is positive word of mouth. When people are talking about your brand in a positive and excited way, it's a good sign that your brand strategy is relevant and on track, or at least in the right place at the right time and top of mind. When no one is noticing or talking about your brand, it's time to get busy. Buzz creates awareness. Awareness creates Interest. Interest creates Desire and Desire leads to Action, or sales. You have to get people talking if you want to get them to buy, and you want them to have a positive buying and product experience that they will talk about with their friends and contacts.

Like a true electrical system, your Motivational Energy cannot last a lifetime without maintenance and improvement. The infrastructure needs to be periodically assessed, updated and adjusted to reflect a constantly evolving marketplace and to meet your own changing life situation and goals. Stagnant brands die. Static brands fade away. Living, breathing, dynamic brands thrive. Bright, shining brands succeed — and they grow brighter every day. Choose to be dynamic.

Keep Your Bulb Burning Brightly: Avoid Burnout

Why do some people shine more brightly than others? What makes them seem more powerful, more successful, perhaps even more attractive? As your bulb grows brighter and stronger, your energy will have a growing impact on the world around you. You will shine brighter and you will add energy and light to a room when you enter it – energy and light that comes from strength, purpose and power.

And people will notice.

Attraction Marketing is a very powerful concept and it will make you a more powerful person in all of your relationships. Power is a perception and it is a positive, productive outlet for your energy; a way to take action, to improve the world or the marketplace, and to help yourself and others move forward. It should never be about domination or manipulation, and it shouldn't have to be. Attraction Marketing creates power that outshines the competition and it is *magnetic*, because it is strength based and market focused. People will be drawn to your light. You will not have to hit them over the head or drag them. They will be naturally attracted to your energy.

Power comes from confidence and attitude. It comes from knowing what you want and what you're good at and using that knowledge to get the most out of life. Channeling your Motivational Energy and utilizing it to its fullest potential creates power and presence, energy and light. You will shine brighter, act more surely and move forward with purpose. Others will naturally be attracted to the magnetic quality of your light.

This ability to attract others and potentially influence them must be accompanied by a sense of responsibility. Access your personal energy and power to shine your brightest and always strive to be the very best that you can be but keep in mind that it is the *balance of power* in personal and professional interactions that creates the most beneficial and productive relationships. Dominating a relationship — whether at home, at work or in the marketplace — is rarely productive and can be blinding to yourself and others. There is no such thing as a one-sided relationship. The very word relationship implies a symbiotic give and take. And: Input is critical to maintaining your light. You must stay in tune and be fully aware of what is happening around you to avoid being blind-sided, side-tracked or even burned out.

It is also important to remain grounded. Power, like money, can be intoxicating and it can divert you from your real goals. Staying grounded requires staying in touch and in tune with the world around you, and being confident but not cocky. Keeping two feet on the ground also ensures that your energy remains positive and that it doesn't become erratic or misguided. We often see celebrities who cannot deal with their fame or visibility. They start acting erratically and appear to burn out quite quickly. We see others who let power go to their heads and abuse it, effectively turning their positive energy into a negative force that repels others, rather than attract them.

In a light bulb, burnout can sometimes be quite spectacular. When a bulb's filament breaks, an arc forms and the current flowing through it becomes unpredictable. As the voltage increases, the arc grows hotter and becomes unstable. This instability can draw even more current, blow the bulb's internal fuse and take out the bulb — and possibly even the dimmer switch or outlet that it is connected to.

You can avoid burnout by staying focused on your Core Strengths and by tending to your Motivational Energy. Build relationships with other powerful, bright shining people. Surrounding yourself with the physical and intellectual energy of other positive people will keep your light burning brightly and help your brand stay strong. It is also important to periodically assess your progress toward your goals and to survey the road ahead. Don't miss the journey on the way to your destination. Take time to experience, enjoy and learn something from every step you take. It is the only real way to move forward.

As you grow and evolve, your goals will also change and your definition of what success looks like is likely to change with them. At some point you may be tempted to think 'I have made progress. This is good enough.' *Good enough is not a goal and it is usually an invitation to inertia.* Stopping to assess the situation, check on your direction and refuel your Motivational Energy is one thing; settling for less than what you originally set out to achieve is quite another. If your vision of success has changed, change your strategy with it. If your vision of success remains intact, take a deep breath, check your compass, rally your resources and keep on. A plateau is not a goal, it is a place to rest while you survey the area around you to see where you are headed next. Growth, evolution and continuous improvement are Motivational Energy builders and Bulb brighteners. Change your pace from time to time, but always choose to be moving forward or building your light in some way.

Frustration can also lead to burnout. If you are investing a lot of energy toward achieving your goals but are not moving forward as fast as you'd like to, stop and check your Source and your Conduit. Conduct periodic 'power checks' to ensure that you are projecting the right type of energy and aiming it at the right type of targets. Measure your 'amps' by checking your Motivational Energy against your day-to-day activities to see if you are on track and actively working toward your goals. Is the road you're on taking you in the right direction? Does it lead to where you want to go or have you stepped off the path along the way? Is your light as bright as it should be or does it appear to be dimming? Is your brand still relevant? Is it still strong? Has the marketplace changed and, if so, have you changed with it? Do those changes jive with your original goals? Questions like these will help you identify factors that may be slowing your progress. Taking time to assess the situation is time well invested. It will ultimately move you further, and faster, toward your goals. Or: You may determine that your goals have changed or identify a new target market or Ideal Customer. Regular assessment will enable you to recognize new information and acknowledge new insights in a timely manner, so that you can make necessary adjustments to your strategy and utilize your Motivational Energy in the most productive way possible.

And remember: Every idea is a spark that can light up your world and the world around you. Ideas are opportunities and opportunities are doorways to success. Be open to the opportunities around you and use your brand's power and light to invite them, embrace them and build on them. It is what entrepreneurs — and powerful, magnetic people — do best.

Chapter 13
Create a Chandelier: Make It All Work Together

I have covered a lot of topics in this book and how they apply to both personal and product brands, in both your personal and professional lives. It could have easily been two books, one on personal branding and one on product marketing, but the principles are so similar that it made sense to keep it all together for several reasons. It is more powerful for you to recognize the common denominators of branding people, products and companies, whether you are a marketing person (or an entrepreneur) or not. Also: Few brands exist in a vacuum. Most are related to at least one other brand. And: *Being the Bulb!* is a total life strategy. It is ideal for entrepreneurs, but it is also highly effective in building more supportive personal relationships. Attraction Marketing is a powerful concept that you can use to improve every part of your personal and professional lives, regardless of who you are and what you do. Understanding its global, whole-life application is important to knowing just how powerful it can be to *Be the Bulb!* It is also the foundation of a total life-work strategy that I call Holistic Entrepreneurship.

Holistic Entrepreneurship is a reality where work and life become true extensions of each other in a productive, beneficial, self-feeding way that fuels your Motivational Energy, instead of draining it. It is way of living, working, growing and succeeding where each element propels the others forward and the business that we create and build is a true reflection of who we are, what we want to give to the world and what we are hoping to get back from the world in return. And yes, you can make money practicing Holistic Entrepreneurship and doing what you love — lots of it. Here's one reason why: When you are doing something that you believe in, when you have created a business that is built on a concept that you are interested and passionate about and that is truly built on your Core Strengths, you will invest more time and effort into making it successful. The quality of the time and effort that you invest will also be of a much higher caliber. You will embrace your work, your business and your life and be excited about it.

And it will embrace you in return.

Holistic Entrepreneurship

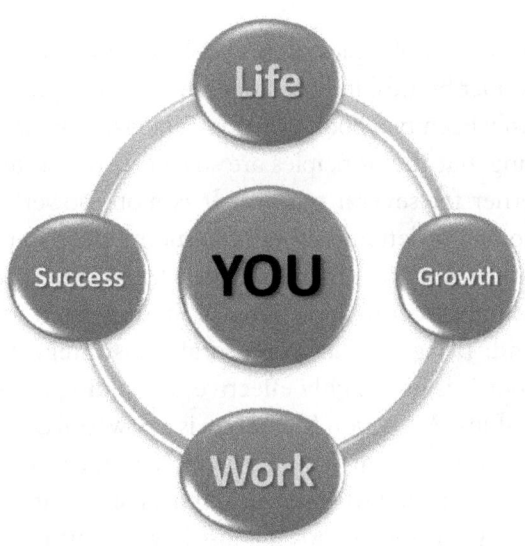

Attraction Marketing is the foundation of Holistic Entrepreneurship. It recognizes the power of your Core Strengths and utilizes them to create a Source of Motivational Energy that lights up every part of your life. It makes it possible for you to reach out and attract what you want and need to be successful, to bring it toward you and to build on it. When you are happy, satisfied and feel successful in one area of your life, it is going to carry over to the other areas (and relationships) of your life and make them brighter and more powerful. You can not *Be the Bulb!* unless you have intimately linked your personal strengths, interests and passions with your professional goals (and vice versa). It is both a requirement and the reward: whole-life personal and professional success is Holistic Entrepreneurship.

In other words: Being all that you can be, in every part of your life.

Create a Chandelier: Make It All Work Together

And that can be a lot. Each of you has a personal brand, whether you acknowledge it, or work at it, or not. Often you will have to manage company and product brands on top of your personal and professional reputations. This can become quite a balancing act (and very stressful) if the different aspects of your life do not share a common sense of purpose and direction. Each should be aligned with your Core Strengths in some way. The multi-armed 'chandelier' of your life is made of many parts, but it all stems from one Source, your Core Strengths, and it is all driven by one power source: your Motivational Energy. When all of the elements are working together and each of the individual 'bulbs' is burning brightly, a chandelier is a beautiful sight to see. It is also a very powerful provider of light and a focal point that draws eyes — and attention — toward it.

Focusing on your Core Strengths is what turns every day into a new growth and learning opportunity. Work becomes exciting, inspiring, fulfilling and productive. Synergies seem to be everywhere around you, but they are actually being generated from *within*. When you are being true to your Core Strengths, and using Attraction Marketing to project your Motivational Energy and reach out to the world and the marketplace, everything feels possible and anything *is* possible. Each of us is filled with energy and ideas and potential. Your Motivational Energy is the spark that can light up your world and the world around you. Attraction Marketing channels that energy, directs it and propels it toward your goals to move you forward and to draw what you want closer. Attraction Marketing draws its power from an inexhaustible supply of Motivational Energy that you self-create and generate. It is not reliant on a bank loan, a partner's agreement, expensive equipment or any other outside influence. You create it. You direct it. You control it and you nurture it. It is a very personal way for an entrepreneur to accelerate his or her achievement and success, and it is a very productive and powerful way for any person to *assure* that they are realizing their full potential. *You can do this.*

Attraction Marketing combines elements of personal branding, target marketing and proven marketing principles with the power of intention and the energy of active effort. It CAN be learned. I have explained the theory and the process and shown you the steps that you must take to *Be the Bulb!* Use them.

Attraction Marketing puts your light and your energy in the path of people who can help you succeed. They will notice it and be drawn to it. This will create opportunity and synergy — and success.

You will get back what you put into the marketplace. Your Motivational Energy must be genuine, and it must genuinely reflect your Core Strengths and your goals and intentions. Invest the time to create a true Source that is based on what you want and need, not what others want and need from you. Build a Conduit that is focused on your goals. Lay the groundwork and take the time to prepare *before* you Flip the Switch and put your strategy to work. Make sure that the road that you have chosen is the road that leads to where you really want to go. Then get started.

Entrepreneurs are especially well-suited to capitalizing on their Motivational Energy to create synergy and success that builds on the power of being true to their Core Strengths. (Personal Branding + Company Branding + Product Branding + Total ME (Motivational Energy) = Synergy and Whole-Life Success.) ME provides the energy that fuels your efforts. Active Attention creates and maintains the momentum. Attraction Marketing projects your energy into the marketplace and attracts what (and who) you want and need back to you. This two-way flow of energy (and communication) is vital to attracting and keeping customers, claiming market space and building a successful venture and an absolutely Ideal Situation: Being Successful at What You Love To Do.

Two Positives Keep Things Positive, But Negatives Always Take Away

Being the Bulb! is an active and involved process. You will attract what you ACTIVELY ask for and work toward. It is as simple as that. Active Attention is the Switch that puts Motivational Energy (ME) to work. The good news is that you don't have to buy anything — or become anyone — other than who you (truly) already are. Your Core Strengths are inherent to who you are as a person. Focus on them and be passionate about what you want. Channel that energy and focus on how your personal strengths and attributes translate to meaningful benefits. Then develop your Conduit

Create a Chandelier: Make It All Work Together

(your strategy) around those benefits and propel your energy and its message into the marketplace. Aim it toward the types of people that you want to attract. You already have all of the resources that you need at hand. *Use them.*

Positive energy attracts positive energy and optimists attract other optimists. Focus on positives and you will bring more positives into your life. Focus on negatives and you will attract more negatives. Author Michael Lozier wrote in his book, *Law of Attraction*, that you should 'Remove your attention from the Don't Wants and place it on the Do Wants'. That's good advice. How you look at life will dictate what you attract and see. If you see yourself as being successful, you will be successful. If you are confident and act confidently, others will have confidence in you. You create your own reality. If negative people or events impact your life, you can control your response. Choose to focus on what you want and need and it will come into your life in abundance. If you doubt this at all, try it for a week and see. A change in perspective and attitude will change your world. It really does begin, and end, with you. If you are not happy with how things are going, you have only yourself to blame. You have the choice to accept things as they are or to take action to make them better. Choose to be happy. Choose to be successful. Choose to *Be the Bulb!*

Attraction Marketing focuses you, your Core Strengths and your Motivational Energy on your desired goals:

$M/E = MC^2$

Step 1 = Identify

Step 2 = Amplify

Conduit 1 = Create Goals and Intentions

Step 3 = Flip the Switch

Conduit 2 = Work the Plan

Step 4 = *Be the Bulb!*

Practice good gatekeeping, active assessment and energy maintenance to avoid inertia, create synergy and keep your Bulb burning brightly. High energy, high visibility professionals and business owners attract energy suckers and other negative people. When you stand up, you stand out. Certain people will always be attracted to that. Gatekeeping prevents their negativity from diluting your positive energy. It keeps your focus where it needs to be: on realizing your intentions and goals.

Negatives take away from positives. They subtract from the quality of your personal and professional lives. The synergy created by combining positives will keep you and your business moving forward. You can choose to work with, collaborate with and hire positive people — or not. You can choose to be successful in what you have chosen to do — or not. You can choose to *Be the Bulb!* — or not.

Choose to *Be the Bulb!* Put the power of ME — Motivational Energy — and what you've learned from this book to work to realize your goals. Banish negatives from your language, your brand and your life. Channel your Motivational Energy to attract the success that you want and need and to add something positive and enduring to the community and the world:

ME as a person;

ME as a professional;

ME as an entrepreneur and a business owner;

ME as an employee;

ME as a leader; and

ME as a member of my industry, my community and my world.

$$M/E = MC^2$$

Be the brand. Be focused, committed, consistent and proactive. Put yourself in the path of success and *Be the Bulb!* Creating, promoting, protecting and nurturing a brand based on ME will lead to entrepreneurial success. Harnessing multiple sources of complimentary, positive energy will lead to exponential growth. True life and work synergy (not balance, but self-feeding, self-propelling synergy that creates momentum) will come from focusing on your Core Strengths and creating a reality that is built from them, not just on them. Holistic Entrepreneurship is a total Life/Work Strategy that brings all of the pieces together in a way which makes you excited to wake up and jump out of bed each morning, regardless of what you have to do. When you are 'in the circle' and *Being the Bulb!*, your world view changes. You will see every challenge as an opportunity and realize that every seeming obstacle has been placed in your path for a reason. It deserves a closer look to find the opportunity that may be hidden within.

Put Yourself in the Path of Success

You have to create your own opportunities for success. Life is full of opportunities that will present themselves to you on a daily basis: people you stand or sit next to, chance meetings, unplanned events, items seen or read, offered projects, ideas that seemingly come out of nowhere. You must recognize each of these occurrences for what they *can be* if you use them to achieve your goals. Opportunities exist to help you move forward, often by presenting a path that you had not considered before. Be open to them.

And choose to put yourself in the path of success, always.

Look for opportunity around you and then leverage it into something more. Watch for it. Evaluate it. Answer the door and build on it. Don't let it pass you by. That's the true 'secret' to success: being actively aware of and open to opportunity. Successful people are not just open to opportunity, they actively watch for it. They are waiting, and watching, and when they see it, they reach out for it and embrace it. They don't wait for success to happen. *They make it happen, one opportunity at a time.*

Just as you have to put yourself in the path of people who can help you achieve your goals, you have to put yourself in the path of success. We often hear about being 'on the road to success'. There is no one road to success, but there are a lot of paths and side roads. Many paths will take you to the same place. Some will be faster, some will prove to be lengthy detours, and others will be dead-ends that don't bring you anywhere near your goals (or at least you won't think so at the time, but that's another story ...). Knowing which path to take is where both intuition and strategy come in — intuition from being true to your Core Strengths; strategy from building a Conduit that is properly directed. Side trips also help you develop and grow. Knowing when to step off the main road and explore a new path is where both courage and creativity come in. Knowing when to stop exploring and accelerate for a while to get closer to your destination is where *experience* comes in. Experience is what you gain when you embrace opportunity, assume risk and take action. Like opportunity, it is essential to success.

Opportunity is out there. If you are open to it and actively working toward your goals, it will find you. Better yet: Put yourself in the path of success by focusing on what you want to achieve. Immerse yourself in your topic. Think about it, read about it, talk about it. Tell others about your goals, with passion and enthusiasm, and they will also become more real to you. Look for learning opportunities. Watch for related information and read it. Go to events, whether they seem to be directly related or not. Follow your instincts. Things cross our path for a reason. Reach out to people, talk to people, follow up with people who cross your path, even if it is only briefly. *Actively look for and create opportunities to be successful and you will be successful.*

We are all familiar with the saying: 'Follow the path and see where it leads.' Opportunity is a path. It is a potential side road that can move you forward, or prove to be the true path to achieving your goals. Be aware of and open to possibilities and *then act on them.* Some will pan out, others won't. But you will never know what COULD have happened unless you follow the path of opportunity for a while. *In order to truly be open for business, we have to be open to opportunity.*

Be the Bulb! and be successful — in business, in relationships, in life. Yes, some people really do shine brighter than others. Now you know how to become one of them.

Epilogue

Chapter 14: Epilogue
A Million Watts of Energy

How Writing this Book Brought My Bulb Back To Bright

This book was a long time in the making. Well, not this book exactly, but my first book. I have been planning to begin for many years but, as I'm sure you know, life often gets in the way of getting to where we truly want to be. I have taken quite a few side roads on this journey of mine. Some were just a brief detour or scenic route, others proved to be a longer, much harder course. All of them, however, proved to be valuable paths to take. I learned something from every experience, sometimes the hard way, adding another piece to the woman, the entrepreneur, the consultant and the author that I have become.

It was just about ten years ago that I realized the power of my light. It had been functioning off and on my entire life without my realizing it. Sometimes it shone very brightly. Other times it was dimmed to nearly nothing as I found myself on an especially dark and difficult road — a time when I no doubt needed it most. It came into its own in the late 1990's, or perhaps I just acknowledged its existence for the first time in a very long time. My business was ten years old and had always done well. I invested my new-found energy and enthusiasm into promoting myself and my company in a way that was true to what I needed and wanted it to be and the results were extraordinary. My volume doubled in the first year and the quality of the clients whom I began to work with increased dramatically. I was involved in the community, writing a weekly column for the newspaper and running a successful sole proprietorship that was supporting myself and my children, building retirement and college funds and providing income for two employees. More than a decade later — my company turned twenty years old last year — I am still doing what I love: consulting, creating, presenting and writing. Every day is different and interesting. Every project is challenging. My Bulb is burning very, very brightly right now.

Just a few years ago, I couldn't really have said that. I had just moved to Arizona from Illinois and I was taking a stab at 'slowing down', thinking that it might be time to pull back the work schedule, spend more time making friends and relaxing and 'planning' to write my first book. I let my light dim, thinking 'that was then and this is now', and not realizing that my Bulb had as much to do with me as a person as my company, my career and my work.

I am one of those individuals who literally lives and works at the speed of light. I am always on the go and happiest when I am busy and juggling a number of different projects and interests at one time. (I call it 'plates in the air'.) Slowing down and trying to live life at a different pace did not work for me. I missed the challenges, the interaction, the success and the applause. I began networking, working my way into the local business community and building my visibility in my new home city. I suggested new projects and strategies to my existing clients and increased my workload with interesting, challenging new work. I sought out writing and speaking opportunities and began travelling (literally) down a whole new path, which I am still just beginning to explore. My Bulb is burning brighter than ever now and it feels good. It feels right.

Writing this book played a big role in making that happen, as I re-focused my attention on my own Core Strengths and what I really wanted and needed in my life. Writing is essential to who I am. It always has been. So is teaching, leading and motivating. This book is providing me with opportunities to put those strengths and talents front and center, where they belong. It is intended to be the first of many such efforts. I was born to write and to encourage others to great success. I hope you agree.

So many synergistic things happened during the months that it took for this book to take shape. People and opportunities appeared at almost every step to encourage me and fuel my efforts forward. I started a new company with a partner to develop and present workshops around the country. Our weekly meetings to talk about our individual and combined work and lives helped keep me focused on my goal to get my first book written. Mary listened to my theories and ideas and then pulled back while I was writing and not really willing to talk about it. I knew that she would celebrate my success when I finally finished the first draft. Thank you, Mary.

I spent seven months working one day a week as a small business development center counselor in downtown Phoenix. I had counseled aspiring entrepreneurs at a community college before leaving Illinois and missed the challenges and rewards of helping small business owners plot their own success stories. My revisited counseling experience reminded me how valuable my knowledge and experience can be in helping others find their own paths. It is an amazing feeling when you can see the proverbial 'light bulb go on' over someone's head after you have explained a concept or made a strategic recommendation and you realize that they 'get' it.

About two thirds of the way through the first draft of this book, I began to let life get in the way again. I took on more work, more projects and more speaking opportunities and I left myself with very little time to write. Opportunity, however, kept knocking at my door. I dated a man who had written a book and met some of his friends who had also published. I began reading new topics and authors and began thinking, in depth, about energy, opportunity and how the combination of the two is so empowering. I read about archetypes and realized that I have always been a Nurturer, a Teacher and a Builder/Developer. This combination of three describes me exactly and is the foundation of what I want to do with my life. Archetypes are the building blocks of Core Strengths. They are intimately and irreversibly linked to each other.

I plunged forward, making writing the first thing that I did every morning. I broke the project down and tackled it in pieces. It is far less daunting to write an 'essay' and then add it to the book, then to sit down and write a book in its entirety. I built a career out of writing for other people this way. I applied a very marketable talent that I had developed and put it to work on my own project. I became my own best client and gave myself, and my project, the same attention and exceptional service that I would give to any company or community on my client list.

The entire effort has been a tremendous learning experience, as much of my life usually is. I am so excited to be where I am right now: turning the page on the next chapter of my life's work and my life's story. It is a work in progress and always will be — as I am, and as you are also.

Long story short, I thought that I had packed my professional Bulb away, but it turned out to be temporary storage. I have been very fortunate to have built a career and a company on doing what I love to do. Very few people can say that. I was not being true to my Core Strengths when I tried to stray from that path. I was trying to fit myself into the pace and lifestyle of my new Arizona neighborhood without paying attention to what was right for me. This time, however, circumstances and opportunities collaborated to keep me from taking a detour. (More likely, I was just paying better attention to myself and the world around me. In the past, I would often go charging off, despite what the universe was trying to tell me.) I am now on the path that I am meant to be on at this time in my life. My Bulb is burning very brightly, my eyes are fully open to opportunity and I can see where I am headed.

And this time, the road is taking me directly to where I want to go.

Being the Bulb! is not a once-in-a lifetime strategy. *It is a whole life lifetime strategy.* Once you have experienced the light, it is impossible to go back to darkness. *Be the Bulb!*, beginning today, and watch the rest of your life light up — for the rest of your life. You have the power to make it happen. Us it well, and use it wisely.

About the Author

Author Lori Martinek's multi-faceted marketing and management experience (agency, corporate, media, academic and non-profit) has made her a sought-after branding strategist and consultant. As a successful serial entrepreneur who owns an award-winning marketing and public relations firm and an independent publishing company, Lori knows how to inspire — and help her clients create — personal and organizational success.

Lori is an accomplished speaker and a consultant and coach to CEOs, small business owners, community leaders and elected officials. She has counseled new and expanding businesses and is a former president, board member and adviser to chambers of commerce, economic development groups and non-profit ventures.

Lori holds a Master's Degree from Northwestern University's prestigious and highly competitive Medill School of Journalism and a Bachelor's Degree from the University of Wisconsin - Madison, Vilas School of Journalism. She has served as a new business development and marketing counselor for SBA-funded Small Business Development Centers (SBDC) in both Illinois and Arizona.

The author built a successful marketing firm from the ground up and today it serves a national client base. Lori's other publishing credits include articles on management and marketing for national publications and bylines in metro newspapers. *Be the Bulb!* is her debut book.

You can learn more about Lori at www.pplusonline.com, at www.herlifepublishing.com and at her author's page on www.amazon.com.

Order additional copies of this book at www.herlifepublishing.com. Email publisher@herlifepublishing.com for quantity discounts.

Email Lori at bethebulb@herlifepublishing.com

Notes

Notes

Notes

www.ingramcontent.com/pod-product-compliance
Lightning Source LLC
Chambersburg PA
CBHW071713090426
42738CB00009B/1764